ASIA-CHURCH IN MISSION

ASIA-CHURCH IN MISSION

Exploring *Ad Gentes* Mission Initiatives

of the Local Churches in Asia

in the Vatican II Era

James H. Kroeger, M.M.

CLARETIAN PUBLICATIONS

ASIA-CHURCH IN MISSION: Exploring *Ad Gentes* Mission
Initiatives of the Local Churches in Asia in the Vatican II Era

Copyright © 1999 by **James H. Kroeger**

A division of Claretian Communications, Inc.
U.P. P.O. Box 4 Diliman, 1101 Quezon City, Philippines
TE: 921-3984   Fax: 921-7429
E-mail: claret@cnl.net   Website: http://www.cnl.net/claret

Claretian Publications is a pastoral endeavor of the Claretian Missionaries in the
Philippines. It aims to promote a renewed spirituality rooted in the process of total
liberation and solidarity in response to the needs, challenges, and pastoral demands
of the Church today.

Cover Inspiration: Donald R. Delgado

Library of Congress Cataloging-in-Publication Data

Kroeger, James H., 1945-
     ASIA-CHURCH IN MISSION: Exploring *Ad Gentes* Mission
Initiatives of the Local Churches in Asia in the Vatican II Era /
James H. Kroeger.
       p. 143   cm. 21 X 13.4
       ISBN 971-501-853-X

    1. Missions—Asia.   2. Catholic Church—Asia.
    3. Catholic Church—Missions—History—20th Century.
    4. Catholic Church—Synods—Asia.   5. Catholic
Church—Bishops—Asia.   I. Title.

       BV2185.K912   1999
       266.023—K912   CIP

CONTENTS

PREFACE

The Second Vatican Council has variously been described as "the key or pivotal religious event of this century" and "the most important occurrence in the history of the Roman Catholic Church since the Protestant Reformation." Emile Poulat has noted that the Church saw more changes in only two post-Council decades than it had seen in the previous one hundred years.

The *aggiornamento* program of Vatican II has impacted both the Universal and local Churches in all aspects of life and ministry. Within this broad context, the essays, studies, and documentation in this book take a unique focus. They aim to capture highlights of the "missionary *aggiornamento*" in Asia's local Churches—on the eve of the third millennium. What are the missionary initiatives and activities of the local Churches in that part of the world which in previous times was called "the Far East"? How has the Church in Asia imbibed the dynamism of Vatican II and rededicated herself to evangelization, particularly *ad gentes* mission?

The presentations comprising this work are divided into three thematic sections. Part One, focusing on the growing mission consciousness of Asia's local Churches, begins with a narrative chronicle of recent developments in Asian *ad gentes* mission. This historical panorama is followed by the statements of two recent colloquiums of Asia's missionary societies. A lengthy chapter introduces the six "Asian-born" *ad gentes* missionary institutes, giving a current overview-synthesis of these evangelizing communities. A brief final chapter presents Church structures and organization that enhance missionary cooperation and assure greater mission effectivity; significant signposts and pertinent bibliography are noted.

Part Two takes up the insights on mission from the 1998 Special Assembly for Asia of the Synod of Bishops, popularly known as the "Asian Synod." Four authors each present both general and specific insights drawn from this month-long reflection process by the bishops of Asia. One chapter is devoted to a synthesis of the dominant mission themes surfacing in the Synod. The subsequent chapter outlines the challenges of mission in contemporary Asia. Insights on the "soul of mission" form another chapter. Finally, two pivotal Synod statements are presented; they clearly impact mission initiatives in Asia.

The third part of the book is formed by three rather distinct items that are relevant to mission in Asia. A chapter is given to current Asian mission statistics and the challenges they pose. A second piece provides a lengthy panorama of the Federation of Asian Bishops' Conferences (FABC) inspiring thought on the local church, which they consistently call "the acting subject of mission." A brief list of contact information for Asia's indigenous mission groups concludes the presentation.

Several pieces included in this book have been published by the Federation of Asian Bishops' Conferences (FABC) in their ongoing series entitled: FABC Papers; the selected essays appeared in FABC Papers No. 88 under the title: LIVING MISSION IN ASIA: Recent Initiatives of Local Churches for Evangelization.

As noted earlier, these various short essays molded into eleven chapters aim to capture the "missionary aggiornamento" as it is emerging in Asia's local Churches, now crossing into the third millennium.

James H. Kroeger, M.M.
Mission Sunday –1999

Part One

MISSION CONSCIOUSNESS IN CONTEMPORARY ASIA

CHAPTER 1

ASIAN *AD GENTES* MISSION INITIATIVES

RECENT DEVELOPMENTS

Tracing the lines of the Holy Spirit's action in Asia—that is the purpose of this essay. How are the promptings of the Spirit being manifested in the *ad gentes* missionary activity of Asian-born mission societies? Already one can perceive a "faith-statement" in the very purpose of this presentation. It is the firm belief of this writer that the Holy Spirit is clearly active in Asia's local Churches and in their concrete, evangelizing initiatives for bringing the Gospel into all strata of Asian life and society.

In the Vatican II era, a Spirit-filled epoch in the Church, six Missionary Societies of Apostolic Life have emerged in Asia; they are: Mission Society of the Philippines (1965); Missionary Society of Saint Thomas the Apostle—India (1968); Catholic Foreign Mission Society of Korea (1975); Missionary Society of Heralds of Good News—India (1984); Mission Society of Thailand (1990); Lorenzo Ruiz Mission Society—Philippines (1997).

Each of these missionary institutes has a very unique history [refer to Chapter 3]; however, all share several commonalities: they are Asian-born; they emerge in the Vatican II era; they are committed to *ad gentes* mission for life and reflect a specific charism: Missionary Society of Apostolic Life. Their unique identity and contribution is *Ad Gentes*, *Ad Exteros*, and *Ad Vitam*. They direct their efforts of evangelization *ad gentes* (to those who have not yet heard the liberating and salvific Good News of Jesus Christ), *ad exteros* (to peoples outside their own country, cultural milieu, and language group), *ad vitam* (through a life-long commitment to this unique form of missionary witness).

Mission societies with the identical charism have long prospered in the Church, the oldest being the Paris Foreign Mission Society founded in 1660. Some other examples are: PIME Missionaries, Maryknoll Fathers and Brothers, Missionary Society of Saint Columban, PME and Scarboro Missioners from Canada. Fifteen such societies of Pontifical Right exist in the Church; most of them continue to serve mission in various parts of Asia. The example and experience of these groups, coupled with a local Church missionary dynamism, have led to the foundation of similar societies throughout Asia—all under the lead of the befriending Spirit.

These Asian-born missionary societies have already made a significant contribution to *ad gentes* mission, frequently offering their services to needy dioceses in the Asia-Pacific area. Papua New Guinea has probably received the most personnel from these Asian societies. Arrangements for personnel, support, and evangelization commitments are common between a diocesan bishop and the individual missionary society. Readers are invited to examine the presentation of each society in a subsequent section to see where and how these Asian missionary personnel engage in evangelization today. As one reads, an inspiring chronicle of faith, service, Gospel witness, and docility to the Spirit will unfold.

NEW INITIATIVES. In the mid-1990s the Office of Evangelization (OE) of the Federation of Asian Bishops' Conferences (FABC) embarked upon an effort to bring the missionary societies of apostolic life indigenous to or working in Asia together for an international colloquium. This initiative was promoted by Archbishop Telesphore P. Toppo of Ranchi, India (FABC: OE Chairman), Father Sebastian Karotemprel, SDB (FABC: OE Secretary), and Father Edward Malone, MM (FABC Assistant Secretary General). The vision of the organizers of the colloquium was to enhance missionary effectiveness and cooperation among all the missionary societies of apostolic life serving in Asia.

The initial gathering of thirty-three missionary-participants was held in Thailand on April 2-6, 1997; it was Easter Week, a most appropriate moment to reflect on the mission mandates of the Risen Lord: Go forth. Teach all nations. Be my witnesses to the ends of the earth! The colloquium provided an opportunity for these evangelizers to share their vision and experience of "Mission in the Orient" and their "Gospel Option for Asia." The five-day exchange became a fruitful experience of missionary renewal and cooperation.

Archbishop Toppo opened the colloquium, noting that the gathering need concern itself "with the vast continent of Asia, with its immense multitudes of people dear to God." He continued: "Catholics in Asia constitute a tiny minority. Yet we know they are called to be the light of the Asian world and the salt of the Asian earth. The primary responsibility for spreading the faith in Asia rests on Asian Catholics, first and foremost."

Observing that "the time has come for us to raise our eyes beyond our limited horizon and to cast our glance over the whole of Asia," Archbishop Toppo said that "Asia needs to be shalomized and evangelized.... It is in this context that we have to consider the matter of Mission Sending Societies. They are the God-inspired instruments of the Asian Church's outreach in love to the millions."

Fraternal greetings to the colloquium participants were received from Jozef Cardinal Tomko, the Prefect of the Congregation for the Evangelization of Peoples: "As I greet all the participants of this very special Asian Conference..., it is my hope and prayer that, following in the heroic footsteps of so many other missionaries who came to Asia in the past, you will take up with ever greater vigor and spirit this truly missionary charism of mission *ad gentes*." Msgr. Luigi Bressan, Pronuncio of seven Asian nations, paid a brief visit and addressed the assembly, expressing the urgency of mission in Asia through a creative use of statistics and mission data.

MISSION IN CONTEMPORARY ASIA. Two major papers were presented to initiate the discussion at the conference. Father Sebastian Karotemprel, SDB, gave an overview of the Missionary Institutes of Apostolic Life. Father Raymond Rossignol, MEP, Superior General of the Paris Foreign Mission Society, presented his "musings" and learnings drawn from his Society's 336 years of missionary endeavors in various Asian countries.

Karotemprel highlighted several items: Even though each local church is responsible for evangelization, "the role of Missionary Institutes has not diminished.... The age of Missionary Institutes is not a matter of history but of urgent actuality.... Collaboration in mission has, therefore, become very crucial for the very existence and continuance of mission today.... The missionary experience of the older Missionary Institutes will also be a valuable guide for the younger Asian-born Missionary Institutes." Indeed, the conference enhanced such beneficial interchange among the "older" and "younger" Asian Missionary Societies of Apostolic Life.

Rossignol, musing over more than three centuries of missionary service in Asia, spoke of the Paris Foreign Mission Society history and territorial evangelization in Asia, learning languages, sharing the life of Asian peoples and local churches, the establishment of seminaries for the formation of local clergy, pastoral activities, and the formation of new Churches. Admitting mistakes and failures and thankful for successes, Rossignol noted: "There is obviously an element of mystery in the way God runs His mission.... Mission work remains essentially God's work."

Each of the twelve participating mission societies were afforded the opportunity of presenting their mission society, its history and Asian experience, current commitments, learnings and reflections. The four Asian-born SALs, each represented by its Superior General or Father Moderator, were given first priority: Fr. Ruben C. Elago, MSP of the Mission Society of the Philippines; Fr. Sebastian Vadakel, MST of the Missionary Society of St. Thomas the Apostle (India); Fr. Bonaventura Jung, KMS of the Catholic Foreign Mission Society of Korea; and, Fr. Jean Dantonel, MEP of the Missionary Society of Thailand.

Various Missionary Societies of Apostolic Life that serve in Asia sent delegates to the colloquium (they ranged from superior general or general council members to long-term field missioners). Represented were: Paris Foreign Mission Society, PIME Missionaries (originating in Italy), Catholic Foreign Mission Society of America (Maryknoll), Spanish Foreign Mission Society, Quebec Foreign Mission Society, Bethlehem Mission Society (Switzerland), Scarboro Foreign

Mission Society (Canada), and the Congregation of the Missionaries of the Holy Family.

A noteworthy fact is that missionaries and diocesan clergy from Asian countries that do not as yet have a foreign mission society were also in attendance: Bangladesh, Cambodia, Hong Kong, Indonesia, Japan, and Taiwan. This panorama of mission-focused Asian church-persons produced an extraordinarily rich exchange—to the credit of the organizers of the colloquium. The experience showed that whenever missionaries gather, dynamism and enthusiasm emerge because evangelization and mission are placed center-stage, "our special priority"—in the words of one participant.

COLLOQUIUM STATEMENT. A brief statement was crafted which captures the highlights of this first international gathering of the Asian Missionary Societies of Apostolic Life (the group popularly called itself the "ASAL Conference"). The final statement gave prominence to several themes: (1) proclaiming the Gospel in Asia as a new millenium dawns; (2) gratitude to God for the missionary vocation; (3) rejoicing at the growing missionary dynamism of many local churches in Asia; (4) a vigorous recommitment to the unique SAL mission charism that is *ad gentes, ad exteros,* and *ad vitam;* (5) affirmation of theological foundations of mission and promotion of genuine missionary qualities; (6) establishment of an "ASAL Desk" under the FABC Office of Evangelization with Maryknoll Father James Kroeger requested by Archbishop Toppo to head this endeavor; (7) finally, a series of concrete suggestions aimed at promoting "the proclamation of the Gospel in the Asian context." These seven topics are a mere listing of the major themes of the colloquium; thus, readers are encouraged to view the full Colloquium Statement presented in Chapter 2.

Participants expressed their gratitude to the FABC Office of Evangelization for its initiative in organizing the gathering. They admitted that the colloquium had the strengths and limitations of an initial, organizational conference. The body expressed its strong desire that the role of missionaries in Asia would be adequately represented at the Special Synod of Bishops for Asia. Friendships were formed; commitment to *ad gentes* mission was affirmed; mission experiences, joys, difficulties and dreams were exchanged; faith, prayer, and liturgy integrated the experience.

Throughout the week-long gathering, spontaneous, insightful comments were frequently heard: "Every local church is too poor to think it can manage by itself, and every church is so rich that it has something unique to share." "Maybe it is time for us as missionaries to pass from the option for the poor to the option for non-Christians—and the second option doesn't deny the first." "It struck me that the founders of several missionary organizations had a very lively Eucharistic spirituality." "All mission necessarily includes mystery and elements of poetry."

CONTINUED COLLABORATION FOR MISSION. The positive and enriching experience of the April 1997 colloquium was shared with members of the respective mission societies. The nascent ASAL Organization began functioning to strengthen relationships and communication among ASAL members; the modest ASAL *News* began publication [it was subsequently incorporated into PROCLAIM, the newly established quarterly newsletter of the FABC Office of Evangelization]. Some members published short articles in various languages about ASAL and mission *ad gentes* in the Asian context. The proceedings of the 1997 Thailand assembly were edited by Sebastian Karotemprel, SDB and published by the FABC Office of Evangelization in a book entitled: *Heralds of the Gospel in Asia: A Study on Missionary Institutions in Asia.* The ASAL secretary-convenor began his work to enhance cooperation and communication within Asia and with similar societies in other continents.

Mission and Evangelization in the local Churches of Asia again came to center stage during the Synod of Bishops Special Assembly for Asia (April 18 - May 14, 1998). ASAL concerns reached the floor of the "Asian Synod," particularly through the intervention of Father Edward Malone, MM on April 24, 1998 [see Chapter 8]. "Proposition 28" in the final list of 59 propositions noted: "This Synod recommends the establishment within each local Church of Asia, where such do not exist, of missionary societies of apostolic life, characterized by their commitment exclusively for the mission *ad gentes, ad exteros* and *ad vitam.*" In addition, it was recognized how Pope John Paul II had taken special note of this Synod theme and incorporated it into his 1998 "Message for World Mission Sunday" (Section 5).

The existence and purpose of the ASAL organization is to foster and facilitate *ad gentes* mission in the Asian context. The approach is one of missionary animation and voluntary collaboration. Thus, each missionary society retains its own autonomy; ASAL claims no legislative or decision-making role. Partnership-in-Mission remains an ideal for ASAL members.

The ASAL organization of Asian missionary societies has now coordinated its rhythm of gatherings with the established pattern of other groups in Europe and the Americas. International colloquia are held in the even-numbered years; continental colloquia fall on the odd-numbered years. Four ASAL persons and the ASAL secretary-convenor participated in the international assembly held in Dublin, Ireland (April 25-30, 1998); this was preceded by a special week-long session on "Formation for Mission" in London for the formators of missionary societies.

SECOND CONTINENTAL COLLOQUIUM. The missionary vitality of the local churches in Asia was again experienced in a unique way as all six of the Asian-born Missionary Societies of Apostolic Life (AMSAL) gathered in Tagaytay, Philippines for their continental colloquium (August 17-21, 1999). This event marked the first time in history that Superiors-General and General Council personnel of all the AMSAL members were able to participate; the earlier organizational gathering in Thailand in 1997 had brought together some members of these indigenous Asian missionary societies. The purpose of the 1999 AMSAL Colloquium was to explore how these missionary movements could better facilitate *ad gentes* mission in Asia in the approaching third millennium.

Archbishop Jaime Cardinal L. Sin of Manila received the participants at his residence on the first morning of the colloquium. The Cardinal, a close friend of missionaries and a strong advocate-supporter of the two indigenous Philippine mission societies, spoke of the permanent need of the Church for selfless missionaries—especially for Asia and foremost for China. In addition, he described the national mission congress being planned for the Philippines in the year 2000; he emphasized the centrality of the family for missionary vocations and the importance of active recruitment for mission societies.

The working sessions of the five-day colloquium reflected on the mission insights and agenda that emerged from the 1998 Synod of Bishops for Asia: what does *ad gentes* mission mean in the challenging context of Asia; how do missioners realistically address Asian realities (demographics, peoples, cultures, religions, ecology, globalization, socio-politico-economic situations, etc.); how are missioners to be heralds and proclaimers of faith and redemption in Jesus—all in the context of great respect and reverence for the values, faith convictions, and freedom of conscience of everyone?

Although the majority of the input and exchange was among the twenty-one participants, two speakers, who attended the Asian Synod, were invited to address the assembly. Archbishop Gaudencio B. Rosales, DD presented his paper "The Soul of Mission"; he focused on the spirituality of the proclaimer within the Church's mission of love and service in Asia. Father Luis Antonio "Chito" Tagle, member of the Pontifical International Theological Commission, spoke dynamically on "The Challenges of Mission in Asia: A View from the Asian Synod." As a colloquium participant, Archbishop Petrus Turang of Kupang, Indonesia, who also was present at the Asian Synod in Rome, shared several additional Synodal insights; [refer to Chapters 6 and 7 for the Rosales and Tagle presentations].

CONCRETE MISSION INITIATIVES. The colloquium did not remain on the level of theoretical explorations. As is common in all gatherings of missioners, practical questions were addressed: How are mission locations chosen and personnel assigned and prepared for mission? What kind of formation is needed to instill a creative and pioneering spirit in the missioner? How do the mission societies promote their *ad gentes* charism—especially when there are many pressing pastoral needs? How does one recruit and animate for mission in the local church of origin? How is the *ad gentes*, *ad exteros*, and *ad vitam* commitment promoted in young people and in the missioners themselves?

An additional recurring theme in the colloquium focused on areas of missionary cooperation. Participants received copies of the recent (October 1, 1998) instruction *Cooperatio Missionalis* issued by the Congregation for the Evangelization of Peoples; they explored its meaning for their societies. In addition to direct inter-society collaboration in formation and overseas mission apostolates, the AMSAL delegates affirmed the importance of continued close cooperative links with the Office of Evangelization of the Federation of Asian Bishops' Conferences (FABC: OE). The presence of Saturnino Dias, Executive Secretary of FABC: OE was welcomed; the Secretary affirmed this linkage and spoke of the importance of this collaboration. AMSAL will find its natural link with the "Missions Desk" of the FABC:OE.

Archbishop Marcello Zago, OMI, Secretary of the Congregation for the Evangelization of Peoples (CEP) in Rome, had planned to attend the colloquium; health factors forced the cancellation of his participation. AMSAL affirmed its strong desire to continue close missionary collaboration with the CEP through the person of Archbishop Zago. In addition, the colloquium was enriched by the presence of Bishop Vicente C. Manuel, SVD, DD, Chairman of the Commission on Missions of the Catholic Bishops' Conference of the Philippines (CBCP). Father Pedro Mesiona, MSP, National Director of the Pontifical Missionary Societies—Philippines, was present and spoke about missionary animation in the local church.

AMSAL welcomed the participation of representatives from additional local churches throughout Asia (Bangladesh, Cambodia, and Indonesia); invited delegates from Japan and Myanmar were unable to be present. The purpose of including "non-AMSAL" participants was to encourage mission-minded persons in those Asian local churches to consider their response to *ad gentes* mission. In this context, participants recalled "Proposition 28" from the Asian Synod (noted above) which recommended "the establishment within each local Church of Asia, where such do not exist, of missionary societies of apostolic life, characterized by their commitment exclusively for the mission *ad gentes, ad exteros,* and *ad vitam.*"

A pervasive spirit of joy and missionary enthusiasm permeated the entire five-day gathering. Visits to the Lorenzo Ruiz Mission Society Seminary in Manila and to the Mission Society of the Philippines (MSP) Center in Tagaytay provided opportunities to meet priests and seminarians of the two hosting missionary groups. The visit to the MSP Center included a Eucharistic celebration, followed by a typically Filipino meal and short cultural program presented by the seminarians of the "Fil-Mission" Society; this visit added variety to the more formal colloquium events. These experiences affirmed the truth that missionaries must be "joyful evangelizers" (Paul VI) in order to effectively communicate the Good News.

COLLOQUIUM STATEMENT. The AMSAL-1999 colloquium issued a short statement as a brief summary of its deliberations and discussions [see Chapter 2]. The statement is marked by a renewed commitment to the Church's missionary activity; this commitment flows from the participants' renewed appreciation of their unique charism as *ad gentes, ad exteros,* and *ad vitam* missionary societies of apostolic life. The official acronym of the organization (AMSAL) was augmented from ASAL (adopted at the initial organizational gathering in Thailand in 1997); by including the word "missionary" in the full title of the organization, emphasis is laid on the particular charism of these Asian-born societies: *ad gentes* mission is the heartbeat of these missionary communities.

The AMSAL group will follow the rhythm of assemblies of similar missionary societies in other parts of the world; continental groupings of missionary societies now exist in Europe, the Americas, and Asia. Each society was invited to send a participant to the International Assembly of the Missionary Societies of Apostolic Life to be hosted at Maryknoll, New York (April 29 - May 4, 2000). AMSAL itself plans to gather again on a continental basis in two years. The next AMSAL colloquium will be hosted in November 2001 by the Missionary Society of Saint Thomas the Apostle in India. The theme for the next colloquium will be: Missionary Spirituality and Formation. The continued work and position of Maryknoller James H. Kroeger as AMSAL secretary-convenor was unanimously approved by the colloquium participants.

CONCLUSION. This overview has traced some recent developments in the *ad gentes* mission response of Asian local Churches. It is a chronicle—often presented with a fair amount of detail—that documents the continued awakening to mission in the Asian continent. A perceptive observer will clearly see the power of God's Spirit in these seemingly mundane events. The action of the Spirit, the principal agent of mission, is the dynamic force inspiring these movements and renewing local Churches to be in a permanent state of mission.

This chronicle brings one to the opening of a new chapter in the mission response of Asia's local Churches. Pope John Paul II will visit Asia and deliver the post-Synodal Apostolic Exhortation; the third millennium will dawn and demand an expanded mission vision, new methods, and generous, committed personnel. The Church will face many challenging questions and situations. Yet, faith affirms that all will move forward with the caress of the Spirit. *Veni, Creator Spiritus!*

CHAPTER 2

ASIAN MISSION SOCIETIES COLLOQUIUMS

A. THAILAND **ASAL** CONFERENCE (April 2-6, 1997)

The Office of Evangelization of the Federation of Asian Bishops' Conferences organized a colloquium for the representatives of the Asian-born missionary societies and those others working in Asia, at the Redemptorist Center, Pattaya, Thailand, from April 2-6, 1997 to study their common commitment to the announcement of the Gospel on this vast continent at the dawning of the 3rd millenium. Twelve Societies of Apostolic Life (SAL) were represented.

The participants of the colloquium expressed their gratitude to God for the great vocation that their institutes had received in sharing the mission of local churches in the proclamation of the message of Christ to other peoples, establishing and nurturing to maturity Christian communities in different parts of Asia and beyond. They rejoiced at the growing vitality and dynamism of many of the local churches in Asia that had already become mission-sending churches.

In keeping with the teachings and lived traditions of the older missionary societies, the new ones too joyfully affirmed that their commitment was to taking the gift of the Gospel to those who had not yet heard about Christ, crossing the boundaries of nations, cultures and every other form of barrier. They accepted it as a lifelong commitment (therefore, AD GENTES, AD EXTEROS, AD VITAM).

They realized the importance of profound convictions about the theological foundations on which their calling was based and the strong spiritual motivations that would continue to inspire them.

They looked forward to stirring up missionary zeal both in the local churches and among the members of their own institutes, and raising up active young members with genuine missionary qualities: prayerfulness, charity and generosity, detachment, austerity of life, adaptability, respect for peoples, religions and cultures, availability, courage and optimism, simplicity of manners and authenticity.

They gratefully accepted the offer of the FABC to help them by establishing a desk of ASAL under the FABC Office of Evangelization, to facilitate relationships among their societies.

Reaffirming their commitment to mission and evangelization and their unique SAL identity and with the goal of enhancing the proclamation of the Gospel in the Asian context in a coordinated way, the participants expressed their hope that several of the following would be achieved:

1. Continued communication of mission experiences, methods, opportunities, and resources; this could partially be accomplished through an ongoing newsletter for all Asian SALs; this newsletter would be edited by the ASAL societies themselves and be published twice a year.

2. Regularly scheduled meetings and Colloquiums; yearly gatherings would be held: (a) in odd-numbered years on an

Asia-wide basis; (b) in even-numbered years on a world-wide basis with all SAL groups.

3. Ongoing reflection on the unique SAL charism of *ad gentes* mission. This would include mission spirituality, mission theology, and careful selection of apostolates.

4. Sharing of personnel resources among SALs, particularly those qualified in areas of spirituality and missiology.

5. Mutual cooperation of SALs in implementing concrete responses to mission needs in the field and undertaking common *ad gentes* mission in needy places.

6. That ASAL will assure proper representation at both national and continental levels so that the unique charism of SALs will be understood and appreciated.

7. The continued relationship of SALs indigenous to or working in Asia within the ASAL group.

8. Continued mutual relationship between ASAL and FABC.

9. A renewed commitment of SALs to mission animation and promotion in both the local churches of origin and of current apostolate. This calls for a close relationship with our Church of origin. It also demands a sensitivity to the missionary and pastoral plans of the dioceses where they are serving.

10. That as an expression of the missionary nature of the each church, Bishops' Conferences explore the possibility of establishing similar mission organizations or institutes in those places where presently none exist.

B. PHILIPPINE **AMSAL** CONFERENCE

(August 17-21, 1999)

COMMITMENT TO MISSION IN ASIA
FOR THE THIRD MILLENNIUM

Representatives from all six of the "Asian-born" Missionary Societies of Apostolic Life (AMSAL) gathered from August 17-21, 1999 in the Betania Retreat House in Tagaytay, Philippines. This AMSAL group was joined by delegates from some other local churches of Asia and from a few foreign Mission Societies and the Executive Secretary of the Office of Evangelization of the Federation of Asian Bishops' Conferences (FABC). The focus of this five-day colloquium was to explore mission in Asia at the dawn of the new millennium, and the discussion drew upon the key mission themes and agenda emerging from the 1998 Synod of Bishops for Asia.

The fact that this was the first time in history that all six "Asian-born" societies came together was a special joy for the participants of the colloquium. These societies are the Mission Society of the Philippines, Korean Foreign Mission Society, Mission Society of Saint Thomas the Apostle (India), Lorenzo Ruiz Mission Society (Philippines), Mission Society of Thailand, and Heralds of Good News (India).

* *

We superiors-general and other delegates of the AMSAL Colloquium, after deliberating on the concerned issues, wish to make the following observations and commitment:

1. Conscious that the originality of our Mission Societies is *ad gentes, ad exteros,* and *ad vitam,* we took stock of the following realities of Asian countries: that over 50% of the world's population resides in Asia; that Catholics in Asia are only a small minority of less than 2% (the Philippines is the only predominantly Catholic nation); that the majority of poor people live in this continent; that Asia is the birthplace of the five major religions of the world (Hinduism, Buddhism, Islam, Judaism and Christianity); and, that there is the variety of deeply-rooted living cultures in Asia.

2. With this background, we see the urgency of the implementation of the missionary mandate of Jesus Christ and hear the call specially addressed to us as Mission Societies *ad gentes.* We realize that:

    a. Jesus who came as a messenger of the love of God our Father is himself the Message of Life and must be proclaimed in word and life;

    b. Our message is that it is through his death, the breaking of his body and the shedding of his blood, that we receive forgiveness of sins. His death is the expression of the greatest love of God for us. Therefore, he is the only Savior of the world.

    c. This message, which is being conveyed through our instrumentality by the same Jesus and the Holy Spirit, who is the principal agent of mission, will be effective only if we witness to it through our life.

    d. This message of the love of God the Father can best be proclaimed in the context of multi-religious and pluri-cultural Asia and prevalent poverty of its peoples through the mode of triple dialogue with the religions, cultures and poor among whom we live.

Therefore, we commit ourselves:

1. To take every opportunity to make Jesus Christ and his message known in a way that is acceptable to Asians, presenting him to them with an "Asian Face," using Asian cultural concepts, terms and symbols.

2. To learn about the other religions and understand cultures, taking the Incarnation as our model.

3. To present the Gospel message as humble servants of the Kingdom of God, always sensitive to the religious and cultural traditions of the people where the Spirit leads us to make Jesus known.

4. To strive to be transformed by a life of prayer and contemplation into presenters of Jesus Christ, the kind, compassionate, true and divine master.

5. To inculcate this spirit and the specific charism of our Mission Societies in all our future proclaimers throughout their formation period.

6. To be supportive of each other both through regular meetings and apostolic collaboration in the mission areas where two or more of our Mission Societies work.

We present this our commitment through Mary, Queen of Apostles, to Jesus and the Holy Spirit, who is the principal agent of mission, ready to be led by this same Spirit where he wills.

CHAPTER 3

SIX ASIAN *AD GENTES* MISSIONARY INSTITUTES

In the Vatican II era under the guidance of the Spirit, six indigenous missionary societies of apostolic life have emerged in Asia. Although each of these missionary communities has a unique and inspiring history, they share some common elements. All are Asian-born; they emerge in the Vatican II era; they are committed to *ad gentes* mission for life and reflect a specific charism: Missionary Society of Apostolic Life.

Three characteristics describe the identity and contribution of a missionary society of apostolic life: A*d Gentes*, A*d Exteros*, and A*d Vitam*. Such societies direct their efforts of evangelization *ad gentes* (to those who have not yet heard the liberating and salvific Good News of Jesus Christ), *ad exteros* (to peoples outside their own country, cultural milieu, and language group), *ad vitam* (through a life-long commitment to this unique form of missionary witness).

A. THE MISSION SOCIETY OF THE PHILIPPINES

The formal establishment of the Mission Society of the Philippines (MSP) dates back to the mid-1960s; yet, the seeds of its foundation are found in the 400 years (1565-1965) of

interaction between Filipinos and Christianity. History
identifies 1565 as the beginning of the effective colonization
and systematic evangelization of the Philippine Islands; the
country has a long history of receiving missionaries from
various parts of the world.

EARLY MSP BEGINNINGS. The seed of faith needs to
sprout and grow. The strong interest in mission among the
local hierarchy led them to state on Pentecost Sunday: "We
decided to set aside the present year of 1959 as Mission Year
in the Philippines." The bishops desired a mission awakening and hoped that "it be said of the Filipino nation...that
they gave freely what they freely received, and that they took
their full share in the work of bringing the joy and peace, the
justice and mercy of Christ to the peoples of Asia."

Five years later in 1964 during the Philippine Bishops'
annual meeting, Bishop Epifanio Surban pursued the idea
of having a Philippine Mission Center as a response to
the local Church's missionary task. In addition, Bishop
Surban proposed the establishment of a Philippine Foreign
Mission Society composed of Filipino diocesan priests.
The proposal was enthusiastically and unanimously accepted.
Bishop Surban was chosen to be the first National Director
of the enterprise; he was requested to enflesh his ideas
and proposal.

The Philippine hierarchy saw that the fourth centenary
of the evangelization of the Philippines (1565-1965) was a
golden opportunity to launch a new evangelization and to
form an indigenous mission society. Their January 29, 1965
pastoral statement formally began the project; they declared:

"Desirous to fulfill our divine commission 'to preach the
Gospel to every creature,' we, the Catholic Hierarchy of the
Philippines, herewith declare our firm determination to share
the light of faith with our...neighbors. It is our conviction

that we as a Christian Nation have reached a mature stage in our four centuries of development and that we are prepared to assume the responsibility of such maturity. We, therefore, proclaim officially our intention to undertake a national effort to orient our people to the Missions. To achieve this and to express in the concrete our gratitude to God for the gift of our Faith we will organize the Foreign Mission Society of the Philippines."

INITIAL MSP GROWTH. A handful of mission-minded Filipino diocesan priests volunteered to be pioneer members of the newly established Society. Although there have been numerous growth pains and uncertainties, the Society has continued. It has experienced its own "dark moments of history" and shared "a lack of sense of direction [that] nearly caused a dissolution." Several bishops have continued their strong support of the MSP; notable among them are Archbishop Gaudencio Rosales and Jaime Cardinal Sin. It has been often affirmed: "God is not yet through with MSP—He has only begun."

The official or statutory name of the society is: Mission Society of the Philippines (MSP), but it is often popularly referred to as "Fil-Mission." As a mission community it has passed several tests of growth; from a handful of volunteer members, its numbers have slowly increased. It averages about four ordinations each year and now (1999) has 65 permanent members.

Over the decades the majority membership has changed from volunteer diocesan priests (early beginnings) to "true, blue-blooded MSP" members (those priests who entered as seminarians and received a solid MSP-designated missionary formation). MSP continues to welcome diocesan priests as associates in mission. The Society defines its charism in these words: "In love and gratitude to the Father, ours is a joyful missionary spirit flowing from deep union with Christ through Mary and in the power of the Holy Spirit, willing to spend and be spent in sharing His Gospel to all."

CURRENT STATUS. From its beginnings, the MSP has desired pontifical status; Rome requested the MSP to begin on the local level. His Eminence Jaime Cardinal L. Sin approved the Society's statutes on January 29, 1988, giving juridical personality to MSP as a Society of Apostolic Life of Diocesan Right and established as such by virtue of the Decree of Establishment on April 25, 1989. Membership in the MSP is open to natural-born Filipinos; the Society also welcomes Filipino diocesan priests as associate members to serve in foreign mission.

The MSP considers its mission apostolate in *de jure* and *de facto* mission territories as its foremost duty and privilege. Although MSP was established with a strong interest in Asia, the movement of the Spirit has also led MSP to work in Oceania and the Pacific Region. Presently, MSP missionaries are working in Taiwan, Hong Kong (China), Thailand, South Korea, Japan, Papua New Guinea, Solomon Islands, and New Zealand.

MISSION SUCCESSES AND CHALLENGES. As a mission society and as servants of the Gospel to Asia, Oceania and the Pacific, the MSP remains enthusiastic and maintains its commitment to share in the universal mission of the Church. This is clearly a strong point and a notable success as a mission society. Words taken from MSP members capture the society's enthusiasm.

"Through the years our contact with the peoples in our mission areas is for us a great privilege. We continuously admire the refined culture rooted in their history which is a clear product of thousands of years of philosophical, religious sense and ways of life, respect for others and nature. Our immersion through the inculturation process in these varied experiences has enabled us to encounter other religions, like Buddhism, Islam and other great religions of Asia as well as the local cult of spirits and ancestors in Oceania and the Pacific. We have been helped to understand new dimensions of our faith. Our missionaries have been privileged to appreciate the positive value of other faiths through different forms of dialogue. As a result, we have noticed a gradual growth and a deepening of our treasured Christian faith."

"Our pastoral experiences in our respective mission areas have rendered us doubly enriched in terms of local culture, traditions, customs, age-old history and even in the dynamism of the young. We find ourselves exhilarated in this upsurge of life. We certainly marvel at the hand of God in all this. We perceive the vitality of the footsteps of God who comes and establishes His reign in the world through the active working of the Spirit who is the life-giver in this great enterprise."

"The sight of these marvels does not blind us to see the face of the Asian and Pacific realities. This is our challenge. A lot of teeming masses are largely victims of poverty. The youth and many of those who have grown up in the so-called post-modern era are confused; they are crushed by a savage economic development which most often debases both humanity and nature. Part of the scenario in these regions is the utter fact of destitution, illiteracy, exploited children and migrants, oppressed women, dehumanized life in the slums and villages, strife and bloodshed in the name of religion, race, tribe and language, suppression of freedom and human rights, and in the background, great economic imbalances. Coming from a country whose situation and experience is no different, it is but natural to have a heart for these people and thus direct our commitment to these challenges."

MISSION PREFERENCES. The MSP seeks to choose locations for mission that reflect its statutory mission commitment. This is an option for: (1) the incarnation of the Church among non-Christian believers through evangelization; (2) supportive evangelical service in favor of young Churches until they attain ecclesial maturity; and, (3) auxiliary apostolic ministry for the renewal of Churches rendered unable to catechize their own people until they achieve ministerial self-reliance.

In the order of priority, the firm MSP commitment is to choose places for mission that specifically provide opportunities for *ad gentes* mission. Within this option, Asia has a special claim on MSP personnel; this choice—without prejudice to other mission areas—is now included as an added criterion for mission placement. MSP consistently receives many more mission invitations than it can accept. There is always the need to evaluate mission commitments; greater mission effectiveness is often the result of consolidated manpower and personal placement.

MISSION IN THE NEW MILLENNIUM. Looking forward in mission in Asia has enabled the MSP to focus on five areas, namely: (1) working for the cause of justice and peace; (2) upholding the sacredness of life, human dignity, and the integrity of creation; (3) promoting interreligious dialogue; (4) engaging in inculturation; and, (5) proclaiming the Gospel. These are not new issues, but they will continue to be the path of mission for MSP in the next millennium.

MSP views its primary commitment as mission *ad gentes*. It affirms its mission "to proclaim the Gospel to all peoples even those beyond our present care." There are standing invitations from Pakistan, Kenya, Tanzania, West

Indies, Samoa, and Uganda. The desire to "expand our wings" is strong; yet, we are "short of personnel." They quickly add: "This should not discourage us to go on and carry out our mission commitment." As missionaries we see "no let-up to the commitment" as we strive to establish "what John Paul II describes as the civilization of love." *Source:* James Kroeger with data supplied by Manuel Jadraque, Jr. (MSP Father Moderator).

B. THE MISSIONARY SOCIETY OF
ST. THOMAS THE APOSTLE

The Missionary Society of Saint Thomas the Apostle (MST) is an indigenous missionary institute of the Syro-Malabar Archiepiscopal Church. It was founded on February 22, 1968 by Mar Sebastian Vayalil, the first bishop of the diocese of Palai, India. As a society of apostolic life, it has the sole purpose of "mission *ad gentes*" in territories and among peoples in which the Church has not yet taken root (cf. AG 6).

EARLY HISTORY. With the reorganization of the Syro-Malabar Church in 1923 under native bishops, there was a tremendous religious renewal and missionary awakening in this apostolic Church. After the independence of India in 1947, there an increase of missionary vocations; about 60% of the vocations that aided mission in India at this juncture originated from the Syro-Malabar Church. This response came quite spontaneously.

All the missionaries carried on their apostolate in the tradition of the *sui juris* Church where they labored. This predicament urged Mar Sebastian Vayalil to embark upon a historic endeavor to begin a new missionary society; it would carry out missionary activity under its own banner and in a manner consistent with the heritage of the Syro-Malabar Church.

In 1960 Vayalil sought the permission of the Holy See to found a missionary society. He received a positive response from the Holy See in 1963, and by 1964 he submitted a draft constitution. He conscientiously kept Popes John XXIII and Paul VI, as well as concerned Congregations of the Roman Curia, informed of his progress; Vayalil actively sought and received their guidance and encouragement.

FOUNDATION OF MST. On the advice of the Holy See, the proposed society began as a Pious Union of Diocesan Clergy in 1965. Pope Paul VI congratulated Vayalil during his *ad limina* visit in 1966 and assured him of his patronage for the Society.

In 1967 the Holy See approved the statutes of the nascent society and authorized Bishop Vayalil to promulgate them and erect a pious union of diocesan clergy as the Missionary Society of St. Thomas the Apostle. The formal foundation of MST came on February 22, 1968 at Melampara, near Bharananganam. It was witnessed by Mar Sebastian Vayalil, Maximilian Cardinal de Fürstenberg (Prefect of the Congregation for the Oriental Churches), Joseph Caprio (Apostolic Pro-Nuncio to India), prelates of the Syro-Malabar Church, and a large number of clergy, religious and laity.

During this foundation ceremony Cardinal Fürstenberg blessed and laid the foundation stone for the Central House and Minor Seminary complex of the Society. Thus, the long cherished dream of Mar Sebastian Vayalil and the diocesan clergy of the Saint Thomas Christians had become a reality.

MST TODAY. The Society, which started functioning in 1968 with eighteen diocesan priests, has grown into a major missionary movement. Today (1999) MST has 227 priest-members, 161 students-seminarians, 3 formation centers, and 3 mission regions.

On the occasion of the silver jubilee of the Society in 1993 the Syro-Malabar bishops through a joint pastoral letter again owned the Society; they exhorted the faithful to extend support to its missionary activities. On July 3, 1997 the revised constitutions of the Society were approved by the Church, and the Society was recognized as a "Society of Apostolic Life of Major Archiepiscopal Right" in accordance with CCEO 572; [equivalently, this corresponds to "Pontifical Right" in the Roman Church].

MISSION REGIONS OF THE MST. The *ad gentes* mission activities of the MST are found in the less Christian regions of India and beyond. The first mission region entrusted to MST was the Apostolic Exarchate of Ujjain (February 22, 1968). Geographically Ujjain is located in the State of Madhjapradesh in central India. The population is 90% Hindu, 8% Muslim, and 2% Jains, Buddhists and Christians. Responsive to the current socio-economic and educational realities in the area, health care, charitable works, social development projects, and education are employed as the means of missionary contact. Mar Sebastian Vadakel, consecreted in 1998, serves as the second bishop of Ujjain.

In 1978 the MST received the Mandya mission district, located in Karnataka in Kerala. Hindus form 90% of the population, with Muslims as the second largest religious community. Agriculture is the main occupation of the people. A wide variety of development efforts are undertaken by the MST, at times in collaboration with the government. There are also outreach services extended to slum dwellers and prisoners.

The largest MST mission territory is the Sangli Mission; it was entrusted to the MST in 1990. Education, health care programs, and AIDS awareness projects are sources of contact with the people. In 1995 the MST took up the challenge of evangelization in Leh-Ladakh, known as the "Roof of the World"; it is a very challenging area for missionary activity. Three valiant MST missionaries serve in this area.

In addition to these geographical mission regions, some MST members render service in several dioceses in India and in Tanzania, Germany, and America. MST maintains a mission animation and communication department to foster vocations and the missionary spirit; they publish *Santhome Mission* each quarter.

APOSTOLIC FRUITFULNESS. Realistically, it may be premature to speak of the fruitfulness of MST. The first MST students were ordained in 1979; they are now in the field for twenty years. They engage in various kinds of charitable activities in the areas of education, health, social development, and work among the down-trodden. Normally, people are appreciative of the missionaries and their sincere efforts. These works are seen to be the early stages of evangelization.

In Ujjain people are willing to join the Christian community, and in some stations there are small baptized groups. The Christian presence and life seem to be positive and bear fruit. Mandya and Sangli are comparatively new and the MST is insisting on non-institutional types of work in the Mandya Mission. The impact of the work is noticeable.

The theological trends in missiology, dialogue, and religious pluralism sometimes influence the missionaries in the field negatively. Changing political situations and religious fundamentalism still make the work of mission *ad gentes* difficult. The recent attacks on Christian communities and missionaries are living realities. Every issue is seen and brought under the banner of religion. The financial burden for the works of evangelization cannot be ignored.

FUTURE MISSION CHOICES. Mission *ad gentes* is the main criterion for MST in accepting mission works and regions. Following this principle, the MST will accept missionary apostolates both inside and outside of India. MST experiences great demands and even pressure to work in established parishes.

As a missionary arm of the Syro-Malabar Archiepiscopal Church, the MST selects areas for long-term apostolate if there is the possibility of following the Syro-Malabar Church traditions. Questions regarding liturgy inevitably arise and must be addressed. It is noteworthy that over sixty percent of the missionaries in India are from the Syro-Malabar Archiepiscopal Church. MST has recently extended the scope of its work to the care of migrants; this is seen as an entry-point for *ad gentes* mission.

The MST is grateful to God for the growth and positive impact of its Society; it has been rendering dedicated service in difficult and even unwelcoming situations. MST believes it can contribute much to Asian countries; it is eager to cooperate with other Asian missionary institutes. The Society has this fervent prayer: "May the Holy Spirit inspire and quicken us to live and propagate the message of Christ in the whole of Asia. Let the future be a millennium of Christ and the Church for Asia." *Source:* James Kroeger with data supplied by Thomas Parayady (MST Director General).

C. CATHOLIC FOREIGN MISSION SOCIETY OF KOREA

The Catholic Church in Korea began with a group of educated Koreans who studied Christian literature they obtained from Peking in 1777. Yi Sung Hun was baptized in Peking in 1783; upon his return to Seoul he soon converted many of his influential friends. So successful was the apostolate of these first converts that when James Chu, a Chinese priest who secretly entered Korea (1794), there were 4,000 Catholics, none of whom had ever seen a priest. By 1801, when Father Chu and 300 others were put to death for their faith, the Church had grown to 10,000.

From the early beginnings when Koreans accepted the Gospel on their own, along with the inspiration of the Korean martyrs and the labors of countless missionaries, the Korean Church has grown steadily. The local Church also became conscious of moving from being a receiving Church to becoming a sharing Church which would contribute to the growth of a world Church.

BRIEF HISTORY. The Catholic Foreign Mission Society of Korea (KMS) traces its origins to late 1974 when a Korean preparation committee was established to explore the possible formation of a mission society. It was the dedicated efforts of Bishop John Choi Jae-Sun that ultimately led to the establishment of the Society by the Korean Bishops' Conference on February 26, 1975.

A formation house was opened in early 1976; the first KMS priest was ordained in 1981. The initial mission departure ceremony was held on November 18, 1981, and the first KMS missionary was sent to Papua New Guinea.

Other significant dates in the KMS journey include the following: March 25, 1986 marked the first Oath ceremony of the Society for both temporary and final commitment; February 12, 1988 saw the beginning of the Spiritual Formation Year; April 5, 1990 was the first KMS sending ceremony for mission to the Hshin-Chu Diocese in Taiwan; the Society began its Overseas Training Program for seminarians on January 7, 1992; the first KMS missionary was sent to Hong Kong and China in a departure ceremony on December 19, 1996.

MISSION VISION. The KMS has expressed its identity and spirit in a variety of inspiring words: "The founding of this Society is a symbol of appreciation for the great grace which God has given to the Korean Church and our sense of responsibility that the Church has for the evangelization of all peoples. Our Society is a sign of a mature Korean Church. We especially have a concern for the world church, so we desire to devote ourselves to a life of mission service for all people. The Society wishes to respond to the needs of the Church especially the Asian Church and the intentions of the Congregation for the Evangelization of Peoples. Our preference is to bring the Gospel message to countries where the Gospel has not been proclaimed or evangelization has not yet been fully realized."

"Taking the command of Jesus Christ, we desire to devote ourselves to the call of mission until the end of time all over the world. The goal of mission which we pursue is to gather into one the scattered children of God (John 11:52) and to advance the time when all people will worship the Father in spirit and truth (John 4:23)."

"Our Society desires to entrust its members to the care of our Blessed Mother, to model ourselves on the evangelical spirit of the Korean martyrs who witnessed to Jesus even unto their death, and to devote ourselves to the work of evangelization for all people through the example of the Korean martyrs. We practice a life of prayer, service, and poverty, in order to be a witness to Jesus Christ, imitating the Apostle St. Paul as a model missionary."

"If charity is truly the spirit that animates the Korean Foreign Mission Society, the result will be unity. There can be no serious progress without unity. There can be no true unity, but only division, without charity. Charity will safeguard unity, and unity will safeguard all of us in fulfilling the divine purpose for which God created the Korean Foreign Mission Society. Only men of charity can be missioners. Only charity can be the spirit of our Society."

CURRENT STATISTICS. The KMS presently (1999) has a total of 66 members; in permanent oath there are 24 priests and two deacons. There are six major seminarians, seven spiritual formation year candidates, and 27 temporary oath seminarians.

Geographically and apostolically, the 24 priest-members are distributed in eight locations with a variety of commitments. Five members are located in the Seoul Center House; they serve as the leadership-administration of the Society. Three missioners are assigned to the Suwon Formation House and one serves the Choam Catholic Church.

KMS members are in six countries outside of Korea. Four missioners are in Madang, Papua New Guinea. Two labor in Hshin Chu, Taiwan, and one is in language study in Hong Kong. Beijing, China is home for two members in language study. Auckland, New Zealand is the assignment for another missioner. Finally, four KMS priests are in renewal courses at the East Asian Pastoral Institute in Manila as they prepare for overseas mission placements.

In recent years the KMS has opted to give much emphasis to both initial and continuing formation for mission. The vision is expressed as follows: "Being based on the spirit of the Korean martyrs and the spirituality of our founder, which is poverty, gratitude, and charity, the purpose of our Foreign Mission Society is the training of members of the Society to realize a humble life style and to devise solidarity and development of a community in imitation of Christ. All are trained for mission by developing their intellectual abilities, good character, and intense spiritual life."

"As *Redemptoris Missio* noted: 'A real missionary is a Saint' (RM 90). Thus, KMS members are enjoined to have a firm faith in the Trinity, the Pascal mystery of the Church, and to place themselves under the special care of our Mother Mary. They have regular personal interviews and spiritual direction to deepen their spiritual life."

"In order to follow the spirituality of Preaching the Message of the 103 Korean martyrs, our Society's patrons, especially the first Korean priest and missionary, St. Andrew Kim, members are urged to read the biographies and study the lives of the martyrs and make pilgrimages to the martyrs' shrines every year."

FUTURE CHALLENGES. The year 2000 will mark the Silver Jubilee of the Catholic Foreign Mission Society of Korea. In a renewed spirit of commitment to *ad gentes* mission in the new millennium, the KMS has enunciated four focused priorities:

1. In response to the needs of the Church, especially the Asian Church and the intention of the Congregation for the Evangelization of Peoples, the Korean Foreign Mission Society plans to open new missions in Cambodia, Mongolia, Central and South Asia.

2. The Korean Foreign Mission Society intends to cooperate with other Mission Societies and mission organizations in developing areas of mutual concern.

3. The Korean Foreign Mission Society hopes to establish an Asian Mission Research Institute and a Center for Missionary Education.

4. The Korean Foreign Mission Society will encourage the Church in Korea to be more mission-

minded and open to proclaim the Gospel to other areas in Asia by accepting diocesan priests through temporary membership.

Mission in the third millennium continues to inspire the missionary outreach of the local Church in Korea through its indigenous mission society. *Source*: James Kroeger with data supplied by Bonaventura Jung (KMS Superior General).

D. MISSIONARY SOCIETY OF HERALDS
OF GOOD NEWS

The Missionary Society of Heralds of Good News is a Clerical Society of Apostolic Life of Pontifical Right. This society of priests was founded by Father Jose Kaimlett on October 14, 1984 in the Diocese of Eluru, India. The objective of the Heralds (HGN) is: "training and supplying zealous, dedicated, hardworking and saintly priests wherever there is need, especially due to shortage of local vocations in the Universal Church." Mary, Queen of Apostles, and Saint Joseph the Worker are the society's patrons.

HISTORICAL OVERVIEW. Father Jose Kaimlett, the HGN founder, possessed a deep consciousness of the shortage of priestly vocations all over the world. He believed that a clerical missionary society of apostolic life could be of great help to the needs of the Universal Church.

In December 1976 the Holy See decided to create the Diocese of Eluru with territory taken from the Diocese of Vijayawada; Father Kaimlett was requested to manage the bifurcation and serve as the administrator of the new diocese. Later Bishop John Mulagada became the first ordinary of Eluru; Father Kaimlett went to study canon law in Rome. His journeys abroad brought him face to face with the priest shortage in many parts of the world, particularly in Western countries.

Dreams for a male missionary institute continued in Father Kaimlett's vision. When he returned to serve the Diocese of Eluru, he received enthusiastic encouragement from Bishop Mulagada to pursue the venture. As a preliminary step he gathered like-minded persons together; three priests and two seminarians expressed their willingness to join the apostolic endeavor.

On October 14, 1984 Bishop Mulagada placed his seal of approval on the Basic Constitution of the Institute. Less than four months later on February 2, 1985, the pioneer members (the Founder, three priests, and two seminarians) made their permanent commitment to the institute.

Additional dates of historical significance for the HGN are: May 5, 1991 (Erection of the Missionary Institute of Heralds of Good News as a Clerical Missionary Society of Apostolic Life of Diocesan Right); November 2, 1994 (Inauguration of the First Province of HGN, the South Indian Province); May 5, 1999 and the 58th birthday of the founder—Father Kaimlett (HGN was raised by Pope John Paul II to a Society of Pontifical Right).

PRESENT REALITIES. The HGN Society has made rapid progress both in the area of personnel and on the level of apostolic activities. Within God's providence, HGN has grown in fifteen years (1984-1999) to have 109 permanently incorporated members; about one-half work in India, the others labor abroad. The Society has 607 seminarians at different levels of formation. All members are expected to contribute actively in vocation promotion activities.

There are many other informative and current (1999) statistics. The HGN has 19 houses (15 in India; 4 abroad),

7 seminaries (2 major; 5 minor) 5 schools, 4 service institutions, and 2 leprosy rehabilitation centers. The Heralds serve in 12 dioceses in India and in 16 abroad (South Africa, Tanzania, Kenya, Uganda, Papua New Guinea, Italy, and U.S.A.). The two major commitments of the Society are in seminaries and social centers—where people can directly experience God's love, compassion, care and concern. Father Kaimlett also founded a female institute in 1992, known as the Sisters of Good News; they currently have 75 sisters serving in India and Italy.

SUCCESSES AND CHALLENGES. The Heralds, in accord with the specific objective of their society, have been particularly successful in the area of vocation promotion, seminary formation, and sending out missionaries. They attribute their success in recruitment to the collective efforts of all society members—especially the seminarians.

The Society has also focused on the missionary spirit and enthusiasm of its own personnel. They happily serve in 28 dioceses around the world. Several bishops continue to request HGN personnel, because of their missionary spirit and earnestness. Requests far exceed available missionaries.

This young mission society, by its own admission, has not yet met any serious difficulties. Their seminary formation initiates candidates into the challenges of future mission; they are readied to accept any sort of arduous assignment. Members are prepared to live in community, and, whenever possible, are assigned with other society members, although there are concrete difficulties in forming community life in some mission locations.

One ongoing challenge is the financial resources needed to meet all expenses. The society has no reserves. It is said: "We trust in the mercy and providence of God. All these years the Lord has been good to us. We pray for our daily bread and the good Lord answers our prayer."

CRITERIA FOR PLACEMENTS. The Heralds admit that they have been blessed with numerous vocations, so "we, as a responsible part of Mother Church, would like to make use of this divine providence for the benefit of the Universal Church."

The only criterion used in the selection of areas of work is "the need and earnestness of the request we receive from the local ordinaries." However, the Society also insists that the local Churches that benefit from their services should share—depending on their resources—some of the formation and retirement expenses of the missionaries.

FUTURE OF MISSION IN ASIA. As an indigenous Asian mission society, HGN sees that "at the approach of the third millennium the Church in Asia is called to renew its understanding of evangelization, which, in fact, has acquired a greater urgency than in the past." HGN affirms that evangelization "consists of a complex reality and as such has many essential elements: witnessing to the Gospel, working for the values of the kingdom, struggle for human liberation and promotion, dialogue, the mutual sharing of God experience...."

Members of the HGN note that "one of the priorities of the Church in Asia is the witness of life.... The first Christians preached the Gospel by the testimony of their lives.... There is no mission without adequate witnessing. Christian mission in Asia is a call for individual and community witnessing in *being* Christ-like as well as *doing* deeds which are Christ-like."

What does it mean to serve in mission in Asia? "The mission of the Church in Asia becomes more meaningful and effective when she identifies herself with suffering humanity. Hundreds of millions of people still live in inhuman poverty. Jesus' concern towards the hungry and the needy and His compassion and love for them must be a guiding principle for all of us. One should not forget that solidarity with the poor, involvement in their struggle for justice, reawakening the consciousness of the society to the needs of the poor and works of charity are all means of expressing integral salvation, which God offers to humanity in Jesus Christ."

As an Asian missionary community, the HGN assert: "In this context of Asian realities the Church is carrying out its mission of salvation. Although the Church in Asia is numerically a small flock, she is called forth to transform every Asian reality through its mission of love and service." *Source:* James Kroeger with data supplied by Philip Kulathinampadickal, HGN and Mathew Kallikatt, HGN (current Director General).

E. MISSIONARY SOCIETY OF THAILAND

The Missionary Society of Thailand traces its beginnings to its first priestly ordinations in the early 1990s. The Society uses the initials MET from the French language, *Missions Etrangères de Thailande;* this is in imitation of the Paris Foreign Mission Society (MEP—*Missions Etrangères de Paris*) that has labored for centuries in this part of Asia.

HISTORICAL OVERVIEW. In March 1987, the Superior of the Paris Foreign Mission Society in Thailand addressed a letter to the Bishops' Conference suggesting the formation of a missionary group of Thai priests. They were to work with the Hill Tribe peoples in northern Thailand. The idea was already present in the mind of some bishops; the Church situation needed such an initiative; there was a great demand among the Hill Tribe peoples themselves. The vision was favorably received by the bishops.

In 1989 Bishop Banchung Aribarg, the Bishops' Conference delegate for this missionary initiative, gathered all those directly concerned with the project. Of those present, a MEP missionary was to initiate something in the Major Seminary; a PIME priest was to contact religious congregations and laity.

At this time four seminarians volunteered to become members of the Society; some sisters and lay persons were also ready to join. One seminarian underwent some specific missionary formation; he was ordained on Pentecost 1990 and during the ceremony he received his mission cross from the Cardinal Archbishop of Bangkok. In January 1991 another ordination-missioning ceremony took place in Udorn diocese. MET sources attest: "we hold that these ordinations mark the foundation of the Missionary Society of Thailand."

These two pioneer members of MET continue to work among the Hmongs in northern Thailand. Additional missionary formation sessions were conducted in 1992, and when Cambodia reopened, MET sent a priest, two sisters, and a laywoman to work there.

MET began functioning without any definite constitution or structure in its early years. The project was under Bishop Banchong of the Bishops' Conference. In 1995, the first provisional constitution was approved for three years. In 1996, the Bishops appointed Jean Dantonel, MEP, as the first superior of MET. The constitutions were reviewed and again approved for three years by the Bishops' Conference. Bishop Banchong has retired and is replaced by Bishop Chamniern Sanitsukniran of Nakornsawan.

CURRENT STATISTICS. The MET is less than a decade old. Other than the superior, the society counts only three priests as full members. Six religious women from three congregations are associate members; five lay persons are with the MET. Currently (1999) a young priest is preparing to join MET; another seminarian has the consent of his bishop to join at ordination time in two years.

Among the members, two priests and two sisters work with the Hmongs in northern Thailand; they have served this mission for eight years. Another priest, four sisters and a laywoman work with the local Church in Cambodia. Two laywomen are at the PIME Center in northern Thailand. Finally, two additional female lay catechists are in the northeast area of Thailand.

Much of the mission apostolate is missionary-pastoral work among the minorities in Thailand. All missioners have had to learn new languages; they collaborate with the local bishop for the formation of Christians and catechumens. Those laboring in Cambodia serve the needs of the local Church in education and catechesis.

SUCCESSES AND CHALLENGES. Judging success is difficult. Membership has practically not increased over the past six years, except for two sisters who joined in 1997. However, in terms of members' work, one sees "real stability and an effective development in their work." Very positive comments are frequently heard on the work and spirit of those with the Hill Tribe people. The MET priest in Cambodia has been named pastor of the Cathedral in Phnom Penh. MET personnel collaborate well with local laity, and the number of catechumens has increased in all mission areas.

It has been observed that there is a "very good spirit of the whole group whenever we have our yearly retreat and meeting... [marked by] a very good exchange among them and a truly fraternal spirit."

The existence and work of MET has impacted the whole local Church. There is a growing consciousness of the necessity of mission work for the Thai Church among seminarians, priests, and religious. MET is frequently invited to present training sessions on the missionary spirit and the urgency of *ad gentes* mission.

Probably the main difficulty or challenge is the recruitment of new members. One may find real interest in mission work, but few are ready to leave comfortable situations and parishes to go to more difficult situations in the Hills or in Cambodia where the people are really very poor.

RATIONALE OF MET APOSTOLATES. The MET constitutions state that the society aims "to announce the Gospel to those who do not know Christ yet, both in Thailand and out of Thailand." In brief, this means that "our main aim is not so much to work *ad exteros* but rather to go *ad gentes*." There is a clear reason for this. The number of Thai Catholics has not increased for the last 50 years; in fact, it is decreasing both in percentage and even in absolute figures.

There is an urgent need to enkindle the missionary spirit within the Church in Thailand, inspiring priests and Christian communities to reach out to those who do not yet know Christ and the Gospel. In addition, there are many areas within Thailand itself that demand of missioners a real change of culture, style of life and language. For Thais from central Thailand to go and work in the North demands a true missionary transformation. Even within the central plain of Thailand, there are many areas not touched by the Church: e.g. the poor, people living in slums. This can be a direct area for missionary work.

In Thailand's neighboring countries, the number of priests and missionaries remains small and insufficient. A clear example is Cambodia. MET also looks with hope to the day when Laos will open its doors.

The MET facilitates lengthy exposure programs for seminarians in mission areas. The results have been positive in the sense that it helps seminarians examine their vocations and view their future priestly life with a renewed spirit.

A clarification is helpful in regard to collaboration with lay people. Based on several years of experience, MET has realized that "we were not properly equipped to give a proper formation or an appropriate work to these lay people." MET is considering "the creation of a sort of parallel branch, especially for lay people." This structure would promote laity in mission, address their unique needs and status, provide distinct rules and constitutions, and facilitate a continued relationship with MET. This is an ongoing, exploratory project.

MISSION IN THE THIRD MILLENNIUM. Although MET is small and it is difficult to present clear perspectives for the Third Millennium, one point remains true: MET needs to promote a distinct opening of the Christian communities towards people who do not know Jesus Christ. This is an important objective for MET within the Church in Thailand; lay people will certainly play an important role in this opening to Thai society.

A mission society must work to help prepare local seminarians and priests for greater involvement in the evangelizing mission of the Church. Priests can do much for *ad gentes* mission—if they are made aware of the possibilities and urgency of missionary work.

MET continues to see the needs of its neighboring countries: Laos and Cambodia. Since the Thai language and culture are very close to the Laotian culture and way of life, MET is in a good position to help the Church in Laos, whenever a concrete opportunity becomes available. Cambodia, too, is still in need of more priests. The MET sees these two countries as the priorities of its *ad exteros* mission work.

It has been noted that the Third Millennium may be the "Millennium of Asia." Thus, an important dimension of mission will focus on the encounter with the religions and cultures of Asia. Very little has been realized in these areas. As an Asian missionary society, MET (along with other Asian societies) is in an advantageous position to foster this intercultural and interreligious dialogue. *Source*: James Kroeger with data supplied by Jean Dantonel, MEP (MET Superior).

F. LORENZO RUIZ MISSION SOCIETY

The Lorenzo Ruiz Mission Society (LRMS) is a Clerical Society of Apostolic Life of Diocesan Right with its ecclesiastical seat in the Archdiocese of Manila. The LRMS draws its inspiration from Saint Lorenzo, the first Filipino saint who was of mixed Filipino and Chinese descent. He was martyred in Japan where he went as a lay catechist with Spanish Dominican friars in the 1600s.

HISTORICAL SYNOPSIS. In 1949 during civil disturbances in China, the Saint Joseph Regional Seminary which was under Jesuit administration was transferred to Manila. In the ensuing years about 60 Chinese seminarians were ordained in the Philippines; they went on to found 14 Filipino-Chinese parishes and 18 Filipino-Chinese schools.

To facilitate the continuation of these apostolates and to recruit and train younger clergy, Jaime Cardinal L. Sin, D.D. of Manila established the Lorenzo Mission Institute (LMI) on June 6, 1987. The LMI is a Filipino-Chinese diocesan seminary and trains missionary priests for the Chinese Apostolate in the Philippines. The first priestly ordination in Bacolod was Esteban Lo (October 16, 1991); next Jose Vidamor Yu was ordained in Davao (January 17, 1993).

Pope John Paul II visited the LMI seminary during his Philippine sojourn for World Youth Day in January, 1995. He instructed Cardinal Sin to "maintain and preserve the said seminary at all cost." The Pope also requested that the Institute not only prepare priests for the Chinese Apostolate in the Philippines but also for mission in China.

It is within this context that the LRMS has been formed. On January 14, 1997 His Eminence Jaime Cardinal L. Sin, on the occasion of the tenth-year anniversary of LMI's establishment, created by special decree the Lorenzo Ruiz Mission Society (LRMS) and approved its constitution. The LMI continues as the formation house of the LRMS.

PRESENT REALITIES. At the dawn of the new millennium (1999) LRMS has thirteen ordained priests, ten theologians, fifteen seminarians in philosophy studies, and one special-English student. Members committed to LRMS are; perpetual (13), temporary (7), novices in their Spiritual Formation Year (5).

Two LRMS priests are in Changchun City, Northeast China, studying the Chinese language in a university setting. One is completing a doctorate in theology in Rome, and another will soon depart for Rome for studies in spiritual theology. The remaining LRMS priests are engaged in pastoral ministry in the Philippines.

The LRMS is "intrinsically and eminently missionary in spirit and finality." Continued discernment is needed for a young mission society to shape its mission commitments. For the present moment LRMS members "will help the Chinese Apostolate in the Philippines, with the evangelization of China in their vision, by living a simplicity of life, giving some special attention to the poor in their pastoral ministry."

The Lorenzo Mission Institute provides a unique and essential service for priests and seminarians from China. LMI has become a kind of coordination center for Chinese Church personnel who come to the Philippines for pastoral exposure, renewal courses, or theological studies. In recent years such assistance has been afforded to seven Chinese priests, two deacons, three Jesuit scholastics, and six seminarians. In addition, three seminarians have come from Taiwan.

SUCCESSES AND CHALLENGES. The LRMS has experienced some initial success in recruitment of personnel. As noted earlier, thirteen men have been ordained; there are an additional seven temporary members and five novices. Recruitment remains a priority for the LRMS.

A distinct challenge emerges from the realities of the Church in China today. It is a divided Church, split between the patriotic Catholic Church and the clandestine or underground Church. The government-patriotic Church must abide by the religious policies of Communist China; it must be self-supporting, self-propagating, and sever all relationships with the Pope concerning the election and ordination of bishops. While the "underground" Church professes fidelity to the Pope of Rome, it is illegal and has no right of existence in China.

In addition, due to the deficiency of theological and pastoral formation of the clergy in China in both churches, constant quarrels emerge between these churches; often, these conflicts have no importance for faith and morals. Unfortunately, there is frequent misunderstanding, and hatreds have even found their way into Church life. There is an urgent need to initiate a movement of reconciliation based on a better understanding of faith and the Christian spirit.

There are three Chinese priests who have spent time at the LMI and have now returned to China. They serve as instruments to slowly foster the work of reconciliation. It is foreseen that in the future additional priests will go to China and join with this necessary movement of reconciliation.

CHOOSING MISSION PLACEMENTS. Presently, China remains closed to missionary activity. There is the possibility of sending priests to China as teachers or students; their activities are very limited. Recognizing these constraints, the LRMS continues to concentrate on the Filipino-Chinese apostolate in the Philippines.

Many Filipino-Chinese commitments were begun many years ago. Currently, there are fourteen parishes and schools. These are often staffed by Chinese priests and missionaries who have reached a retireable age. Serving these commitments meets people's real needs; it is also hoped that they may be a source of vocations.

The vision of the LRMS has a clear focus of "preparing our personnel for the foreign missionary field." The Society does not exclude the possibility of lending a helping hand to the overseas Chinese apostolate if personnel are available. In addition, there is a commitment "to help the seminary formation of the local clergy of China" as soon as China will be open to missionary activity.

THIRD MILLENNIUM MISSION IN ASIA. It is foreseen that over the next 20-30 years China will become more open, and this will enable more mission endeavors. Current Chinese leadership, trained in Communist Russia and the former Soviet Union, will give way to a younger generation. This transition will begin as thousands of young Chinese who studied abroad in Canada, the U.S.A. and other countries come into leadership positions.

This new generation is "fully aware that the communist system will not work." Once they achieve higher positions in the government, they may improve or "even modify the communist system into one that is socialist, like many former communist leaders of Eastern Europe."

The LRMS leadership sees the continued great need of missionaries in Asia in the third millennium. Yet, "there will be surely a shortage of priests and missionaries." This reality means that "the formation of lay missionaries and lay leaders is more urgent today... [because] they shall be the co-workers of the priests."

Specifically for the LRMS, the next decade will include the first General Chapter of its own priest-members with perpetual commitment. This will be an important milestone toward self-governance and stability as an independent missionary society of apostolic life. This expectation emerges from deep faith and trust in the continuing presence of Christ and his Spirit in the Church. *Source:* James Kroeger with data supplied by Paul Lu, PME (LRMS Delegate).

CHAPTER 4

COORDINATION OF CHURCH MISSIONARY ACTIVITY

RECENT DOCUMENTS AND RESOURCES

In its foundation, "the Church on earth is by its very nature missionary since, according to the plan of the Father, it has its origin in the mission of the Son and of the Holy Spirit" (AG 2). Throughout various periods in the Church's history, there have been diverse structures to facilitate the accomplishment of mission. A pivotal event in the coordination of mission effort was the establishment of the Congregation for the Propagation of the Faith in 1622 by Pope Gregory XV (1621-1623). In more recent times— especially in light of the Second Vatican Council—further redefining and restructuring has occurred. This short chapter presents key moments (with only brief commentary or elaboration) which have impacted the Church's mission response in recent decades. A topical or thematic approach is employed for brevity and clarity.

POPES AND ROMAN CONGREGATIONS. Previous to the Vatican II era, the latest reorganization of Roman

administrative structures in this century occurred under Pius
X in 1908. In September 1963 Paul VI addressed the curia
and the Council fathers, noting the importance of structural
adaptation to modern needs. Vatican II recognized the
Pope's "supreme, full, and immediate power" to direct the
Universal Church (*Christus Dominus*). Paul VI moved ahead
with restructuring in his apostolic constitution *Regimini Ecclesiae
Universae* (1967) and the motu proprio *Pontificalis Domus*
(1968). These events affected the entire Church and had a
clear impact on her missionary activity.

Within the general renewal and restructuring of the
Church in the Vatican II era, particular moments and documents affecting mission need to be noted. Growing out of
the debate on implementing the 1967 *Regimini* document, the
directors and consulters of the Congregation for the
Evangelization of Peoples / Propaganda Fide gathered in
Rome on June 25-28, 1968. Two significant documents, both
issued by the Congregation for the Evangelization of
Peoples and signed by Cardinal Agagianian on February 24,
1969, resulted; they are: *Quo Aptius* (Missionary Cooperation)
and *Relationes in Territoriis* (Relations among Local Ordinaries
and Missionary Institutes in Mission Territories).

The second document abrogated for established dioceses
the traditional *"jus commissionis"* (committing a geographical
mission territory to a particular missionary institute for the
purpose of evangelization). Yet, this practice continues in
special missionary areas under a "mandate"; often the term
sui juris is used as the territory is entrusted to a missionary
institute [refer to *"Commissio et Mandatum"* in the bibliogra-
phy]. The focal point of mission activity has now decisively
shifted; the local church and its personnel now bear
responsibility for mission and evangelization ("the acting
subject of mission is the *local church*" FABC V: 3.3.1-2).

Another influential document was the 1978 *Mutuae Relationes* |Directives for the Mutual Relations between Bishops and Religious in the Church|. Prepared in consultation with religious orders and various Vatican organizations and based on the ecclesiology of Vatican II, it sought to better coordinate for greater pastoral efficacy the diverse apostolic charisms and ministries in the Church. *Pastor Bonus* (1988), which accomplished the reorganization of the Roman Curia, outlines the competencies of each Roman Congregation; the Congregation for the Evangelization of Peoples (CEP) is treated in sections 85-92. It is particularly significant that the Missionary Societies of Apostolic Life by their own choice remain under the jurisdiction of the CEP (cf. 90.2).

On the twenty-fifth anniversary of the Conciliar decree *Ad Gentes* (AG), |December 7, 1965 / 1990|, Pope John Paul II issued *Redemptoris Missio* (RM), on the Permanent Validity of the Church's Missionary Mandate. This missionary encyclical dedicates Chapter Seven (Nos. 77-86) to the various forms of "Cooperation in Missionary Activity"; it highlights prayer and spirituality, new forms and approaches, as well as the role of the Pontifical Mission Societies in local Churches. RM achieves a doctrinal-biblical-pastoral-spiritual-practical synthesis of contemporary Church thought and praxis on mission.

The feast of Saint Thérèse of the Child Jesus (October 1, 1998) was the occasion for the Congregation for the Evangelization of Peoples to publish *Cooperatio Missionalis* (Missionary Cooperation). Jointly signed by Cardinal Jozef Tomko and Marcello Zago, OMI, this document has a three-fold objective: (1) to reaffirm the doctrinal principles at the basis of missionary cooperation; (2) to provide concrete guidelines, and, (3) to encourage specific ways of implementing missionary cooperation. The spirit of the Instruction is focused on cooperation and collaboration—all at the service of the evangelization and salvation of the world.

MISSIONARY SOCIETIES. A landmark document entitled "Co-Responsibility in Mission: A S.A.L. Perspective" was published in May 1993. Prepared by the Missionary Societies of Apostolic Life (principal author: Michael McCabe, S.M.A.), this comprehensive document is focused on "a synthesis of the principles governing the relationships between the Missionary Societies of Apostolic Life and the various members of the People of God...and towards the updating of *Mutuae Relationes*." From the perspective of missionary institutes, the document clearly presents the renewal in mission thought and practice in the post-Vatican II era.

The Societies of Apostolic Life (SALs) also provided a comprehensive vision of their charism, life and apostolates for the 1994 Synod of Bishops on Consecrated Life. Only brief mention was given the SALs in the *Lineamenta* (No. 36) for the Synod; *Vita Consecrata* (1996), the post-Synodal document by John Paul II, makes a simple mention of the SALs (No. 11). Such a brief treatment is inadequate for understanding the unique and important contribution that SALs render to the evangelizing mission of the Church. A comprehensive understanding of SALs is facilitated by consulting "Co-Responsibility in Mission: A S.A.L. Perspective" (noted earlier) and the papers from the International Colloquium of the Members of Societies of Apostolic Life held in Ariccia, Italy (November 23-25, 1997).

CANON LAW. The 1917 Code of Canon Law devotes Canon 252 to the Sacred Congregation for the Propagation of the Faith and defines its extensive areas of competence. The 1983 Code treats themes related to mission and missionary personnel in various sections: Institutes of Consecrated Life and Societies of Apostolic Life (573-746); Societies of Apostolic Life (731-746); The Missionary Activity of the Church (781-792). Various Canon Law Commentaries on these sections are now readily available.

PERIODICALS AND JOURNALS. The material on the renewal of missionary life and missionary institutes in the Vatican II era is truly extensive; however, much of it is not available in English. Journals particularly helpful for understanding and documenting the evolution in mission thinking and practice with its concomitant impact on missionary personnel are: *Consecrated Life* (the English-language Edition of *Informationes* published in Rome); *Commentarium pro Religiosis et Missionariis* (Rome); *Omnis Terra* (available from Rome in English, French, Spanish, Italian, and Portuguese); and, SAL *Communiqué* (semi-annual English Bulletin of the Missionary Societies of Apostolic Life).

RELEVANT MATERIALS IN ENGLISH

Bonfils, Jean. "Societies of Apostolic Life (SAL), "*Bulletin: Society of African Missions*. Number 102 (October, 1998), pp. 7-20.

Congregation for the Evangelization of Peoples. >>>"*Commissio et Mandatum* in Mission Territories," *Omnis Terra* Vol. 26, No. 226 (March, 1992), pp. 126-128; >>>"*Cooperatio Missionalis*," *Omnis Terra* Vol. 33, Nos. 294 and 296 (January and April, 1999), pp. 25-30, 169-175.

Degrijse, Omer. *Going Forth: Missionary Consciousness in Third World Catholic Churches*. Maryknoll: Orbis Books, 1984.

Dinh Duc Dao, Joseph. "The Evangelization of Asia: The Challenge of Third Millennium," *Omnis Terra* Vol. 25, No. 214 (January, 1991), pp. 16-26.

Drouin, Pierre. "Institutes of Consecrated Life and Societies of Apostolic Life in the Church and the World" [Lecture given in Rome: November 4, 1994], Photocopied.

Duster, Charles. *The Canonical Status of Members of Missionary Societies of Apostolic Life of Pontifical Right.* Rome: University of Saint Thomas, 1994.

Gay, Robert. "The Role of the Expatriate Missionaries in the Local Church of Eastern Africa," in: Radoli, A. (Ed). *How Local Is the Local Church?* Eldoret, Kenya: AMECEA Gaba Publications, 1993; pp. 163-180.

Karotemprel, Sebastian (Ed.). *Heralds of the Gospel in Asia: A Study on Missionary Institutions in Asia.* Shillong, India: FABC Office of Evangelization and Sacred Heart Theological College, 1998.

Kroeger, James. >>>"Rekindling Mission Vitality and Enthusiasm," *Omnis Terra* Vol. 25, No. 223 (December, 1991), pp. 488-493; >>>"Guiding Vocation Recruitment in Mission," *African Ecclesial Review* Vol. 39, No. 2 (April, 1997), pp. 65-74.

Mascarenhas, Felix. "Societies of Apostolic Life: Their Identity and Their Statistics with regard to the Consecration," *Commentarium pro Religiosis et Missionariis* Vol. 71, Nos. 1-2 (1990), pp. 3-65.

LaVerdiere, Claudette. "Traditional Missionary Institutes Facing New Challenges in Mission," SEDOS *Bulletin* Vol. 29, No. 1 (January, 1997), pp. 25-31.

Maloney, Robert. "The Spirituality of Societies of Apostolic Life," *Bulletin: Society of African Missions* Number 102 (October, 1998), pp. 21-32.

McMahon, Hugh. "The Future of Missionary Societies," SEDOS *Bulletin* Vol. 22, No. 2 (February 15, 1990), pp. 28-31.

Mejia, Rodrigo. "Foreign Missionaries at the Eve of the African Synod," *African Ecclesial Review* Vol. 35, No. 3 (June, 1993), pp. 144-152.

Ombres, Robert. "The Roman Curia Reorganised," *Priests and People* Vol. 3, No. 2 (February, 1989), pp. 59-65.

Rossignol, Raymond. >>>"Vatican II and the Missionary Responsibility of the Particular Church," *Indian Theological Studies* Vol. 17, No. 1 (March, 1980), pp. 34-46; >>>"Societies of Apostolic Life: Their Missionary Dimension," *Omnis Terra* Vol. 33, No. 295 (February-March, 1999), pp. 95-100.

Snijders, Jan. "Bishops and Religious: The Document on the Mutual Relations between Bishops and Religious," *Review for Religious* Vol. 39, No. 1 (January, 1980), pp. 115-126.

Zago, Marcello. >>>"*Redemptoris Missio*, An Encyclical for Asia," *Omnis Terra* Vol. 25, No. 222 (November, 1991), pp. 423-427; >>>"Missionaries for Asia and from Asia," *Omnis Terra* Vol. 30, No. 267 (April, 1996), pp. 148-157; >>>"Challenges facing Religious Life in Asia," *Omnis Terra* Vol. 31, No. 278 (May, 1997), pp. 208-214.

NOTE: The SAL and Church documents cited in this summary-overview, as well as additional sources, are available from: James H. Kroeger, M.M.; Maryknoll Box 285; Greenhills Post Office; 1502 Metro Manila, Philippines.

Part Two

MISSION AND
THE ASIAN SYNOD

CHAPTER 5

ASIA, A CONTINENT OF EMERGING MISSIONARY HOPE

"Asia is truly alive." "Vibrant life pulsates in the peoples, nations, and churches of Asia." "Jesus brings life in abundance for Asia's people." "Life is given as a gift and received as a task and a mission." Such comments capture the enthusiasm that surrounded the celebration of the Special Assembly for Asia of the Synod of Bishops, the "Asian Synod," in Rome (April 18 - May 14, 1998).

A newspaper headline enthusiastically proclaimed: "This is a time of grace when the Church in Asia is called to a fresh missionary outreach" (OR-EE: 4-22-98, p. 1). Indeed, as Pope John Paul II noted in his homily at the Synod's opening Eucharist: the continental synods form part of the "launch of the new evangelization for the third millennium." The pope asserted that for Asia "the new evangelization calls for respectful attention to 'Asian realities' and healthy discernment in their regard" (Ibid., p. 2).

Following a theme from the Acts of the Apostles, the pope set forth the Synod's vision and work: "ours is the task of writing new chapters of Christian witness in every part of the world and in Asia: from India to Indonesia, from Japan to Lebanon, from Korea to Kazakhstan, from Vietnam to the Philippines, from Siberia to China" (Ibid.). The Synod had begun.

The 252 participants began exploring the Synod's theme: "Jesus Christ the Savior and His Mission of Love and Service in Asia: ...that they may have life, and have it abundantly' (Jn. 10:10)." This theme quickly took on pastoral and missionary dimensions: how do Christian communities and local churches really become "Asian Churches"? Clearly, the succinct and helpful expression "a new way of being Church in Asia," popularized by FABC V (Bandung, 1990) and FABC VI (Manila, 1995), provides an interpretive key to much of the Synod's agenda.

"Being Church in Asia" necessarily involves exchanging experiences, needs, faith insights, successes and challenges, personnel and resources. In this whole area of the mutual exchange of gifts among the sister local churches of Asia, the Synod proved to truly be "a UNIQUE EXPERIENCE and a FOUNDATIONAL EVENT" (Final Synod Message, No. 2; OR-EE: 5-20-98, p. 6).

MISSION THEMES IN THE SYNOD

To speak of "being Church" means speaking about a "faith-community-in-mission." Pope Paul VI's inspiring words come to mind: "We wish to confirm once more that the task of evangelizing all people constitutes the essential mission of the Church.... Evangelizing is in fact the grace and vocation proper to the Church, her deepest identity. She exists in order to evangelize" (EN 14). This vision of a missionary Church and its concretization in the Asian context was captured by Indonesia's Cardinal Julius Riyadi Darmaatmadja in his remarks at the Synod's last session: "'Being Church in Asia' today means 'participating in the mission of Christ, the Savior, in rendering his redemptive love and service in Asia ' so that Asian men and women can more fully achieve their integral human development, and 'that they may have life, and have it abundantly' (Jn. 10:10)." The Cardinal also concluded that only through this missionary effort will the Church in Asia emerge as "a Church with a truly Asian 'face'" (OR-EE: 6-17-98, pp. 10-11).

This presentation, a panoramic overview of the mission agenda emerging in the Asian Synod, now turns to a consideration of specific themes. Each thematic represents a particular insight into the integral understanding of mission that surfaced in the deliberations of the Synod.

AN ATTITUDE OF GRATITUDE. Asians treasure the gift of the Christian faith they have received. This appreciation permeated the Synod itself, and several warm expressions of gratitude were publicly voiced. Taiwan's Cardinal Paul Shan Kuo-hsi spoke of "the two millennia of evangelization in Asia, grateful for what has been accomplished." He continued: "thanks to the work of all the 'missionaries' of the past, there is a Christian presence in most Asian countries, and in some countries a very significant presence" (OR-EE: 4-29-98, pp. 7-8). Cardinal Jaime L. Sin of Manila recalled: "Four hundred years ago, European missionaries brought our faith to us. Today our missionaries and overseas contract workers are bringing back this same faith to Europe and to other parts of the world" (Ibid., p. 12).

Father Oscar A. Ante, O.M.F. of the Philippines recalled that "there were countless missionaries who performed wonderful deeds of love and service: sharing of Christian faith; building faith-based communities; adapting the Gospel to the culture; opting to serve the poor through education and health services; witness in martyrdom; and the importance of a simple/poor and recollected/contemplative life-style." He added: "I thank the Lord for the missionaries of the past. They have done their part. Today it is our turn to be open to the Holy Spirit" (OR-EE: 6-3-98, p. 16).

Still in the same vein, one discussion group (English: F) reported that they "thought that the Synod should acknowledge with gratitude the self-effacing labor of all the past missionaries who sowed the seed of the Gospel in Asia" (OR-EE: 6-10-98, p. 13). Indeed, one of the Final Synod Propositions sent to the pope for his consideration in composing an Apostolic Exhortation focuses totally on gratitude. In part, Proposition 58 reads as follows: "The Asian local Churches are deeply grateful.... They wish to express in a very special way their gratitude to all the missionaries, men and women, religious and lay, foreign and local who brought the message of Jesus Christ and the gift of faith. A special word of gratitude again must be expressed to all the Churches who have sent and still send their missionaries to Asia.... We are happy that today some of these Churches are receiving in turn missionaries from Asia."

RENEWED MISSIONARY COMMITMENT. As the Church of Asia swept into Saint Peter's Basilica and the Synod Hall, she brought with her all her wealth and variety of faith, experience, traditions, and customs. She also carried her enthusiasm for being a missionary community. On the very first day of Synod sessions, it was emphasized that: "As the Church in Asia approaches the third millennium, the Synod must serve as a fresh start in a journey leading to internal renewal through an ever greater emphasis on self-evangelization and a renewed commitment to proclaim the saving message of Jesus Christ in word and deed to all the peoples of Asia..." (OR-EE: 4-29-98, p. 7).

The Synod body committed itself to dedicated work: "we want to spend the coming days praying and reflecting upon the mission of the Church in Asia and the new evangelization which is before us.... We want to rededicate ourselves to the mission of the new evangelization in Asia, new in its energy and new in its methods" (Ibid., p. 11).

Archbishop Petrus Turang of Indonesia asserted that: "the Churches of Asia need to develop new missionary endeavors in the context of Asia.... Missionary animation and formation has to be nurtured in seminaries and formations centers.... It is time for the Churches of Asia to revitalize the people's movement on evangelization" (OR-EE: 5-20-98, p. 8).

Cardinal Josef Tomko, Prefect of the Congregation for the Evangelization of Peoples, recalled that Jesus "sent his disciples on mission" and "left the Church a solemn missionary mandate." He believes that "every Christian in Asia can become a missionary of Jesus Christ. And the Great Jubilee of salvation will be the beginning of a great missionary era for Asia under the impetus of the Holy Spirit through this Synod" (OR-EE: 6-3-98, p. 14).

BECOMING EVER MORE MISSIONARY. To assert that the local churches in Asia must become missionary could give a mistaken impression. They are already responding to their inherent missionary identity; statistics indicate that Asia currently sends more missionaries than it receives: 8,147 compared to 5,508 (FIDES: 5-8-98, p. 313). However, the Synod clearly promoted an ever greater commitment to the ideal and practice of mission.

Indian Bishop Ignatius Paul Pinto expressed this sentiment: "Our Christians must become real missionaries. There is a need to instill a genuine missionary spirit in the formation of our Catholics. They are Christians not for their own salvation only, but they have to be signs and instruments of God's kingdom among their fellow men and women" (OR-EE: 5-6-98, p. 9). Bishop Francisco F. Claver, S.J. of the Philippines echoed this theme; he noted that all local communities must be "communities of faith that are truly discerning and prayerful, involved, participative and serious about themselves as a Church in mission" (Ibid.).

Speaking on behalf of his discussion group (English: D), Bishop Ramon B. Villena of the Philippines presented this missionary challenge: "Jesus was born in Asia, and the Scriptures were written in Asia. By our life witness we should evangelize Asians so they can say: 'Jesus has come back to Asia'" (OR-EE: 6-10-98, p. 12).

A BLESSED MINORITY. In all Asian countries except the Philippines the Church is clearly a minority, frequently a very small—even tiny—percentage of the national population. Does this fact negate the Church's missionary potential? Or, is this reality "beneficial" because, as noted by the Jesuit Superior General Peter-Hans Kolvenbach, it forces the Church to examine "the source of every mission: the risen Lord, sent by his Father and who in turn sends his disciples into the whole world." Kolvenbach affirms: "What is important, no matter what the statistics show, is that Christians make Christ and his 'unique mission of love' shine forth" (OR-EE: 5-13-98, p. 14).

The Asian experience has shown that being a minority has value—if it challenges the Church and her members to be more keenly aware of their identity, witness, and mission, to be more authentic bearers, not only of Gospel values, but of the very person of Christ himself. As voiced by Raymond Rossignol, Superior General of the Paris Foreign Mission Society, "no Church is so poor as to have nothing to offer, and no Church is so rich as not to need help from other

Churches." This means that "sending a missionary should not be considered primarily as aid to a poor Church which is unable to be self-sufficient, but as a way of sharing the riches of different Churches for a better service of the mission" (OR-EE: 5-20-98, p. 14).

The minority Churches of Asia are not to be fearful flocks; they are to be signs of hope on the vast Asian continent. In the words of Bishop Leo Laba Ladjar, O.F.M. of Indonesia: "Our master says that we are (and I think we shall remain) a very small flock, *pusillus grex* (Lk 12:32). But he convinces us that we need not be afraid or feel inferior! He himself will be with us always" (OR-EE: 5-20-98, p. 12).

NOT MAINTENANCE, BUT MISSION. Bishop Arturo M. Bastes, S.V.D. of the Philippines, speaking on behalf of his discussion group (English: B), made a blunt and challenging statement: "In many parts of Asia the Church is only in a maintenance mode, not in a missionary mode" (OR-EE: 6-10-98, p. 11). The same assessment was reported from the Italian discussion group (related by Bishop Armando Bortolaso, S.D.B. of Syria): "The Fathers then stress how in the Church of Asia one should pass from the static dimension of preserving her heritage of faith to the dynamic dimension of proclaiming the Word of God, i.e., a new evangelization of Asia is needed in the third millennium" (Ibid., p. 10).

"If the Church in Asia, at the threshold of the third millennium, is called to a fresh missionary outreach," Bishop Joseph Vianney Fernando of Sri Lanka noted, "there has to be a profound soul-searching on how she has to carry out the missionary mandate." He pleaded for a "reorientation in our discipleship of the Lord Jesus in our mission context." Only with a radical rethinking of mission in the Asian context (clearly an underlying theme of the entire Synod) will the Asian Church "cease to be a mere 'maintenance' Church and become a strong force for mission" (OR-EE: 5-13-98, p. 12).

ENGAGED IN MISSION. The overwhelmingly rich and diverse contributions of the 252 participants in the Asian Synod shared, as noted earlier, a common theme: they were focused on the challenge of witnessing to Christ and becoming Church in the diverse contexts of Asia. How can Asian Christians become effectively "engaged in mission"? A brief sampling of some Synod recommendations follows.

Bishop Teodoro C. Bacani of Manila noted: "The fruitfulness of missionary activity depends first of all on the quality of Christian discipleship" (OR-EE: 5-6-98, p. 3). For Bishop Benedict Singh of Guyana, "evangelization must begin within the context of true dialogue which flows into mutual service of the common good" (Ibid., p. 7). "The Church in Asia should proclaim the message of total renewal and integral liberation.... The Church in Asia must also sharpen its prophetic mission so as to prepare Asia for the new evangelization" (Indian Archbishop Joseph Powathil) (Ibid., p. 9).

"In Asia, people believe what they see. People value persons and relationships more than doctrines. In our work of evangelization, we experience how much people value persons and relationships, especially those that embody respect, concern and compassion. Asian ethos of humanity is the first invitation to begin our mission" (Indonesian Archbishop Ignatius Suharyo Hardjoatmodjo) (OR-EE: 5-13-98, p. 11). Echoing this sentiment, Bishop Augustine Jun-ichi Nomura of Japan asserted: "In Japan, like in the rest of Asia, the eyes have a more central role than the ears in the process of insight and conversion" (OR-EE: 4-29-98, p. 13).

"The evangelization of Asia is primarily a dialogue of life with all believers, the experience of which already brings them closer to God.... Mother Teresa of Calcutta showed us, in this way, a path of dialogue with Hinduism and with all Asia's believers" (Vietnamese Cardinal Paul Joseph Pham Dinh Tung) (OR-EE: 6-3-98, p. 14).

In summary, it is validly asserted that at the heart of the Synod's deliberations and of Asia's continued commitment to "being Church" one finds a broad, holistic vision of integral evangelization. This means, as Father Anthony Wicharn Kitcharoen of Thailand noted, "bringing the Good News to all [hu]mankind, through the power of God (Father, Son and Holy Spirit)" (OR-EE: 6-17-98, p. 9). Cardinal Peter Seiichi Shirayanagi of Japan affirmed that, for many parts of Asia, integral evangelization can be concretely and effectively realized through an effort to "understand and appreciate the orientation of the Federation of Asian Bishops' Conferences (FABC). If we were to summarize the orientation of the FABC in one word, it is dialogue" (OR-EE: 4-29-98, p. 13).

In the classic FABC formulation drawn from the First FABC Plenary Assembly in 1974 and quoted on the Synod floor in the *Relatio ante Disceptationem*, "The Church in Asia is called upon to enter into a triple dialogue: a dialogue with the cultures of Asia, a dialogue with the religions of Asia, and a dialogue with the peoples of Asia, especially the poor" (Ibid., p. 11).

ASIAN MISSION SPIRITUALITY. Speaking of mission in the Asian context, home to many world religions, necessarily implies a discussion of mission spirituality, contemplation, prayer, and witness of life. Archbishop Michael Rozario of Bangladesh captured this thematic (found in several interventions): "I would like to speak on the spirituality of the Asian Church in the mission of evangelization.... Those sent on mission must embody the values of the Beatitudes.... Life of witness is a spirituality.... The evangelizer as a person of contemplation and prayer becomes a guru or a teacher of prayer leading people to God.... The missionary embodies the redemptive compassion of Jesus" (OR-EE: 6-3-98, p. 18).

From Indonesian Archbishop Johannes Liku Ada' the Synod heard: "Missionary spirituality in an Asian context would mean readiness and ability to find what is true, good and beautiful in other people of non-Christian religions, even the Spirit at work in them. It should be a spirituality of sincere tolerance and dialogue, harmony and sisterhood/brotherhood.... Missionary spirituality in Asia must be based on the vision of evangelization in an Asian context, i.e., by witness and dialogue rather than by direct preaching" (OR-EE: 5-6-98, p. 10).

The theme of mission spirituality appeared in the Final Message of the Synod: "[Evangelization] calls for a deep missionary spirituality, rooted in Christ, with special emphasis on compassion and harmony, detachment and self-emptying, solidarity with the poor and the suffering, and respect for the integrity of creation" (OR-EE: 5-20-98, p. 6). The same theme surfaced in the closing session of the Synod: "For Asians, Christ is most suitably made known personally, through human experiences more than academics.... The credibility of the evangelizer lies in his or her being a man or woman of God more than a scholar, in being a person who lives simply but with depth..." (OR-EE: 6-17-98, p. 11).

Synod Proposition Eight on "The Joy of Announcing Jesus Christ" speaks of a spirituality for mission. "The Synod Fathers, hearkening to the words of Pope John Paul II, agree to commit all of the Church's energies to a new evangelization and to the mission *ad gentes* (cf. *Redemptoris missio*, 3).... This proclamation is a mission needing holy men and women who will make the Savior known and loved by their lives. A fire can only be lit by something that is itself on fire."

WHO WILL GO? SEND ME. The operative ecclesiology at the Asian Synod was clearly the "total ecclesiology" that emerged from the Second Vatican Council. It is the entire Church (laity, clergy, catechists, religious, and hierarchy) that is missioned to witness its Christian life to the world and embody the values of the Kingdom. "Christian mission is the work of the whole Christian community" (OR-EE: 4-29-98, p. 11).

Within the totality of a missional church, various groups were singled out for the unique contribution they provide: laity, women, religious, youth, and missionary societies. "The laity has an important role to play in the mission of the Church. Many signs indicate that the Spirit is empowering them for an ever greater role in the coming millennium, which could be called the Age of the Laity" (Synod Message) (OR-EE: 5-20-98, p. 7). "The group [English: F] also studied the evangelizing mission of the Church and suggested the need to intensify lay participation in missionary activity and thus the need for the formation of the laity" (OR-EE: 6-10-98, p. 13).

Bishop Peter Remigius from India highlighted the contribution of women: "the role of women in evangelization is clear from the time of our Lord (Jn 20:1-9; Mt 28:8-15; Mk 16:9-15)." Especially responsive to the "condition of women in India, they should be motivated to rise up as the announcers of the Good News" (OR-EE: 5-6-98, p. 10).

Three of the Final 59 Propositions of the Synod emphasized the role of religious, laity, and youth in the mission of evangelization. "Religious orders and congregations have played a major role in the evangelization work of Asia during the past centuries. The Church in Asia is indebted to them and exhorts them to continue the same missionary commitment to peoples of Asia" (Proposition 27). "The laity are important missionaries of the Gospel to reach out to the millions of the Asian people who otherwise might never be reached by the missionaries from the clergy and consecrated life. Catechists have worked wonders" (Proposition 29). Proposition 34, devoted to youth in mission in Asia, reflected the challenge voiced by Mr. Nicholas Somchai Tharaphan of Thailand during the Synod: "As the Church tries to look for a 'new way of being Church in Asia' she will have to learn to walk with young people" (OR-EE: 5-27-98, p. 8).

Very special emphasis was felicitously accorded the Missionary Societies of Apostolic Life in the Asian Synod. A subsequent section of this presentation will discuss this unique contribution to the emergence of Asia as "a Continent of Missionary Hope."

ASIAN MISSION STATISTICS. The challenge of being a missionary church in Asia can effectively be highlighted by understanding important demographical realities obtaining throughout the continent. Statistics often startle; they shake our complacency; they concretize the task at hand: evangelization in modern day Asia [refer to Chapter 9 for an expanded treatment of the brief material presented here].

The largest and most populated continent, Asia constitutes one third of the land area of the whole world; its population is nearly two thirds of all humanity. Catholics worldwide constitute about 17% of all people; yet, in Asia, Catholics represent only 2.9% of the nearly 3.5 billion Asians. Significantly, more than 50% of all Asian Catholics are found in one country alone—the Philippines. Consequently, this leaves very small minorities of Catholics in most Asian nations (cf. OR-EE: 6-3-98, p. 15).

It is noteworthy that 85% of all the world's non-Christians are in Asia; most are followers of several of the world's great religions. Hinduism, born about 5,000 years ago, has about 650 million followers, most of them in India and neighboring countries. Buddhism is a religion and philosophy developed from Hinduism by Siddhartha Gautama, the Buddha (the "Enlightened One"); it has 300 million followers, mostly in Asia.

Islam, established by Muhammad in the seventh century, is a monotheistic religion; it incorporates elements of Judaic and Christian belief. Islam numbers some 700 million followers in Asia alone; the Catholics of Asia are about 100 million. The two largest Islamic nations in the world are found in Asia: Indonesia and Bangladesh—each have well over 100 million Muslims. Other significant religious and philosophical-ethical systems in Asia are Confucianism, Taoism, Shintoism, as well as many indigenous, traditional belief systems (see: *World Mission* [Manila] 8/5: 1995).

These few religious statistics already indicate that "being a missionary church in Asia" demands creative, innovative, dialogical and inculturated approaches to Gospel proclamation. In addition, although beyond the scope of this presentation, one should also consider diverse cultural, political, social, and economic realities in envisioning a pastoral program of integral evangelization. The task before the Synod Fathers was great; they responded with enthusiasm and insightfulness. Recognizing that the Churches of Asia, though numerically small, are a blessed and vigorous minority, the Final Message of the Synod expressed its optimism: "Our greatest reason for hope is

Jesus Christ, who said: 'Take heart, it is I; have no fear' (Mt 14:27), and 'I have overcome the world' (Jn 16:33)" (OR-EE: 5-20-98, p. 7).

NEW MISSION INITIATIVES. It has already been noted that a unique form of missionary witness and service was given special emphasis in the Synod: the Missionary Society of Apostolic Life. In addition to interventions at the Synod, a special Final Proposition (No. 28) highlighted this unique charism.   Pope John Paul II took special note and incorporated this theme into his "Message for World Mission Sunday, which was celebrated on October 18, 1998 [section 5] (FIDES: 5-31-98, p. 380); [refer to Chapter 8 for complete documentation of the synopsis presented here].

On the Synod floor the FABC Assistant Secretary General, Father Edward F. Malone, M.M., spoke of mission realities in Asia and the laudatory contributions of many international missionary institutes of men and women. Then he said: "I wish to highlight a unique and essential form of missionary response—missionary society of apostolic life" (MSAL). Malone noted that "six such societies of men have emerged in Asia." They are: the Missionary Society of the Philippines; the Missionary Society of St. Thomas the Apostle (India); the Catholic Foreign Mission Society of Korea; the Missionary Society of Thailand; the Lorenzo Ruiz Mission Society (Philippines); and, the Heralds of the Good News (India).

Malone pointed out that these groups (MSAL) have a mission charism that is: *"ad gentes, ad exteros,* and *ad vitam"* (see: *Code of Canon Law* 731-746; *Vita Consecrata* 11). Specifically, their contribution is: *ad gentes* (to those who have not yet heard the salvific and liberating Good News of Jesus Christ), *ad exteros* (to people outside their own cultural-language group and nation), and *ad vitam* (devoting themselves to a life-long commitment to this unique form of missionary witness). All are focused on "apostolic" life; they do not pronounce "religious" vows, though they bind themselves permanently (*ad vitam*) for specifically *ad gentes* and *ad exteros* mission.

"The number of societies of apostolic life which are working in Asia is large," Malone continued. "Now it is Asia's turn to give, to be a continent of missionary hope." The gift that such societies are makes them "bridges of communion" and brings many benefits: "Asians evangelizing Asians; the emergence of missionary local Churches; the strengthening of bonds of communion among the Churches of Asia and of 'communion and filial oneness with the See of Peter'" (OR-EE: 5-13-98, p. 14); see also the interventions of Turang (OR-EE: 5-20-98, p. 8), Schleck (Ibid., p. 10), Cagnasso and Rossignol (Ibid., p. 14).

The most direct and concrete mission initiative taken by the Synod came in Proposition 28: "This Synod recommends the establishment within each local Church of Asia, where such do not exist, of missionary societies of apostolic life, characterized by their commitment exclusively for the mission *ad gentes*, *ad exteros* and *ad vitam*." If this and other similar initiatives are implemented in the coming years in the local Churches of Asia, this vast continent will realize its dream to be "a continent of emerging missionary hope."

CONCLUSION. The words of Pope John Paul II at the closing Eucharist of the Synod outline a program of missionary animation: "Dear brothers and sisters, you who have formed the Special Assembly for Asia of the Synod of Bishops! Today the crucified and risen Lord again repeats these same words to you, summoning you once more to evangelize your continent."

"The Church's mission of evangelization," the pope continued, "is a service of love to the Asian continent. And although the Christian community is but 'a little flock' in the total population, it is the means through which God pursues his saving plan.... Dear brothers and sisters, continue this mission of love and service in Asia" (OR-EE: 5-20-98, p. 2).

ABBREVIATIONS

EN   - *Evangelii Nuntiandi*

FABC   - Federation of Asian Bishops' Conferences

FIDES   - International Fides News Service (Rome)

GS   - *Gaudium et Spes*

MSAL   - Missionary Society of Apostolic Life

OR-EE   - *L'Osservatore Romano* - Weekly Edition in English

RM   - *Redemptoris Missio*

CHAPTER 6

THE CHALLENGES OF MISSION IN ASIA

A VIEW FROM THE ASIAN SYNOD

Luis Antonio Tagle

I would like to thank all of you and the organizers of this assembly for the opportunity to reflect once again, with a group of people committed to mission—especially here in Asia, on the significance of the recently concluded Special Assembly of the Synod of Bishops for Asia.

It was a great joy for me to have been invited as one of the so-called "experts" to help in the work of the General Secretariat. Thus, I was given an insight into the workings of the Synod, and I was able to do some work behind the scenes. When the Post-Synodal Council was set up, I was surprised that I was asked to go back to Rome to assist in the Council's tasks. The main work of the Council was to give proposals to the Holy Father for the Apostolic Exhortation which he will promulgate here in Asia.

The topic given me for this presentation is: *The Challenges of Mission in Asia: A View from the Asian Synod.* I will try my best to address this topic and give some sort of introduction to the Synod and its theme. The theme of the Synod itself already gives us some indications regarding the challenges of mission in Asia. I will address some specific challenges or areas of mission as pointed out by the whole Synodal event and by the coming Post-Synodal Exhortation of the Holy Father.

THE NATURE OF THE SYNOD.   Firstly, I will begin with a description of the Synod's nature. The day before the formal opening of the Synod of Bishops, the so-called "experts" were called into a meeting by Cardinal Schotte, CICM, the Secretary-General of the Synod. One of the reminders that he gave us was this: "I am reminding all of you (most of you are theologians) that this is a Synod of Bishops. This is not a Synod of Theologians, and you must clear about that. This is not your Synod. It is not your ideas that must dominate the Synod. You are supposed to help. In other words, this is a Synod of Pastors." From that very identity of the Synod, as a Synod of Pastors, we could already expect that the gathering would be dominated by pastoral concerns.

This fact was verified even in the small group discussions. When an item that sounded too theological or academic arose, the reaction of many bishops would be: "We'll leave that to the theologians to discuss." Then, they would focus on what are more pastoral and more missionary concerns. I noticed that pastoral and missionary were not distinguished in the Synod. So, I will be using the words missionary and pastoral almost interchangeably.

The concern I saw in the Synod was focused on the state of the Churches. Where do the Churches stand in Asia right now, in these many worlds of Asia? The bishops were there in order to assess and to discern the status of our local Churches. In the context of the rich sharing about the state of the Churches, the challenges of mission naturally surfaced.

I will treasure in my heart the many stories which accompanied the interventions of the bishops. No intervention was purely academic; they were always set in context of stories of concrete men and women, concrete Catholics, concrete experiences of local Churches and Catholics. The challenges of mission I discerned were embedded in those stories of life and struggle, of persecution and difficulties, all encountered in living out the faith in different contexts of Asia. That is the first thing that defined this Synod as truly a missionary oriented Synod. It was a Synod of Bishops, of pastors, whose concern was how to promote the mission of the local Churches in the particular context of Asia.

The second element concerns the very theme of the Synod. It was chosen by the Holy Father upon consultation with the Pre-Synodal Council. The various Episcopal Conferences sent representatives to form a Pre-Synodal Council, and they suggested to the Holy Father possible themes of the Synod. Eventually, the Holy Father chose the theme: *Jesus Christ the Savior and His Mission of Love and Service in Asia: "...That They May have Life, and have it Abundantly".* (Jn 10:10). The theme has a rather long formulation and is also quite comprehensive.

Like the themes of other continental Synods (the African Synod, the Synod for America, and the Synod for Lebanon) this also focused on mission and evangelization. The theme of the Asian Synod explicitly mentioned the mission of Jesus Christ. This theme was not chosen in an arbitrary fashion. Much reflection went into it, and I think it is important to pick up some of the nuances. I believe that the nuances of the theme and the history of choosing the theme already indicate some of the challenges of Mission in Asia.

Allow me to highlight a few important points. First, the theme reminds us that it is Jesus Christ who is the Missioner *par excellence*. Jesus Christ is the Missionary; He is the One sent by the Father. I think the theme wants to stress this. Mission is His mission; Jesus is the Missioner. A second nuance was very much in the mind of the Holy Father in choosing the theme: this Missioner Jesus Christ is also the Savior. He is the One Savior, the Only Savior, the Only Mediator between humanity and God. So, Mission, His Mission, the Mission of Jesus Christ, the One sent by the Father, is the Mission of fulfilling the saving plan of the Father. It is a Mission of Salvation. That is why Jesus as Savior was included.

I was told that there were many formulations before this final wording. It started as Jesus Christ as the Only Savior, Jesus Christ as the One Savior, Jesus as the Unique Savior. Then they dropped all the qualifications and just said: Jesus Christ, *the Savior*. The Holy Father stressed that portion: *Jesus Christ in his Mission is Savior.*

The third element is that the description of the saving mission of Jesus is phrased concretely in the theme in terms of *love, service*, and *abundance of life*. Three categories define the mission of Jesus Christ. It is a mission of love. It is a mission of service. It is also meant to bestow life, to share life with the people of Asia. This mission of the Savior is to be incarnated as it were or is to be prolonged in time *specifically in Asia*. The focus of the Synod: how to incarnate this mission of Love, Service and Life in the concrete reality of Asia.

In the experience of the Synod the interventions did not always focus on the theme. The bishops were free to talk about topics of their choice. That is why it was a difficult task for the secretaries. We were in the secretariat and twice a day we had to summarize all the interventions. It was quite difficult because one had to read between the lines. What are the bishops really saying? How are the interventions related to the theme? The connections were not always obvious and not always explicit. It was part of the work of the secretariat not to read too much, but also to try to unpack some of the hidden wealth found in the interventions.

As a gathering of pastors, the Synod was meant to address missionary concerns and missionary challenges in Asia. At the same time, the theme chosen by the Holy Father wanted all to reflect on mission within a particular framework: the Christological dimensions, Jesus as the Missioner, the mission of Jesus as salvific, and all this as concretely experienced in a mission of love, service and life incarnated in the Asia of today.

Of course, what I share with you will not be the final word on this topic. I noticed in the latest issue of *Landas* [12/2: 1998], the Journal of the Loyola School of Theology (Manila), Bishop Francisco Claver and Father James Kroeger had articles on the Synod and specifically on the mission aspects of the Synod. Archbishop Orlando Quevedo had an essay in the *East Asian Pastoral Review* [35/1: 1998] on the Asian Synod and the different orientations and challenges for mission.

THE CHALLENGES OF MISSION IN ASIA. Now let me contribute a little more. I have four specific points. The first challenge that I see based on the theme of the Synod is quite significant: the Churches in Asia are being invited to a humble, discerning stance regarding mission. At the close of the millennium, the missionary fervor that the Holy Father and all the bishops in the Synod wanted to see in Asia is one rooted in the faith conviction that it is Jesus' Mission in the Spirit that must be at work in Asia. It is Jesus' Mission, not ours. It is Jesus' way of fulfilling the Father's salvific plan. It is Jesus' way of concretizing love, service, life-giving love and service. This is the norm for mission. It is Jesus' way. This is one thing that was mentioned over and over again: as we face the third millennium the Churches in Asia must go back to the manner in which Jesus fulfilled His Mission!

The first challenge, I think, coming from the Synod is the basic challenge of learning again from Jesus. We need to allow ourselves to be taught by Jesus, to behold Jesus as the missioner and to be converted. We must undergo this conversion to His ways, to His missionary ways. This first point that I raise is closely connected to missionary spirituality. The Synod stressed that it is His mission. It is not ours; it is His mission. This liberates us a lot.

For discussion during the Synod, we were divided into different small groups. I remember the first three sessions of the small group to which I was assigned. The atmosphere of the sharing was: "This is a problem; that is a problem. How do we address problems?" After the third or fourth sharing and after all the debates, we became more realistic and the atmosphere changed.

One bishop said in our small group, "You know, we are pretending as though we are the ones who will save Asia and we cannot even agree on one particular question like the Inculturation of Liturgy. So how could we be the saviors here in Asia? Maybe the first thing that we can do as people interested in really promoting the mission of Church here in Asia is to be humble and admit that it is not our mission. It is primarily Jesus' Mission. How do we learn from Him?" That liberated our small group. Imagine the weight that our shoulders would have to carry believing that we are the savior. How freeing it was to realize that we just have to learn from the One Who was sent by the Father. I think this is one challenge of mission in Asia: to behold Jesus again. The more contemplative side of mission is to behold Him in order to learn from Him the ways of mission.

The second challenge worth mentioning is this. While it is true that it is Jesus and His mission that are still present, we in the Churches in Asia are being asked to prolong, to make visible, to put flesh unto this mission of Jesus in the contemporary realities of Asia. I do not know whether it is an acceptable or accepted term; this task demands some sort of "contemporalization" of the mission of Jesus Christ within Asian realities. I think the Churches in Asia are being invited to facilitate some sort of encounter, intersection, or meeting between the mission of Jesus which is ever present in the Spirit and the life realities of Asia. That is what the Churches in Asia are asked to do. They are not to substitute for the mission of Jesus, because the mission of Jesus is very much present in the Spirit. The challenge is to facilitate the encounter of the Spirit-filled mission of Jesus with the realities of Asia; in that intersection the mission of Jesus takes on flesh, takes on a form that is contemporary for the people of Asia.

This challenge was expressed in the Synod in different ways. Let me indicate two ways in which this concern for the challenges of a mission surfaced. The first thing that was striking to me was that in the Synod there was a constant call for the Churches in Asia to take seriously and earnestly what Asia truly is. This means to take seriously the different worlds of Asia, because we realized there is not "one Asia." Asia is not a uniform reality. This was a constant appeal in the Synod: "Take the different worlds of Asia seriously and not only in a nostalgic fashion."

You must have seen photographs of the opening and the closing mass of the Synod; they were very colorful. The different parts of the Eucharist were assigned to different Churches. The Gospel was proclaimed, I think, in the Syro-Malabar tradition, and the Alleluia was done in the Syro-Malankara tradition. The presentation of the gifts was done by Indonesians with the dance of three steps forward and four steps backward. The procession seemed to reach the Holy Father after thirty minutes. All very colorful! During the Consecration women from India with flowers and candles were dancing. At the end, all were quite happy that all the different colors, languages, and melodies of Asia were celebrated in that Eucharist.

One Bishop told me, "But you do not see Indian women dancing that way in contemporary India. You do not see Indonesian women dressed that way in contemporary Indonesia." He said, "Why is it that whenever we want to recognize the worlds of Asia we do it in a nostalgic fashion? Why can we not face the contemporary world of Asia?" He asked, "In the Philippines do your women still wear those special dresses?" I said, "No! It is just for programs." He said, "That is it! We are transforming the Synod into a cultural program."

I was surprised, but it got me to thinking. When one says "Be true to the worlds of Asia" it means more than just a nostalgic thing in terms of costume and colors. Are we facing the contemporary worlds of Asia affected by this globalization of cultures and values which has been changing the cultural and the human landscape? What is Asian now? I thought it was a good reminder. When we talk of the worlds of Asia and the cultures of Asia, it is not just a nostalgic view of cultures; the Church must confront the fast-changing, dynamically changing cultures that define the worlds of Asia today.

Why is this true? Because it is in and through these Asian realities that the saving mission of Jesus must be incarnated. So, it is not just for curiosity. We need to know the reality in which the so-called drama is to be played out. The world of Asia is not just a stage. It is a constitutive part of the incarnation of the mission of Jesus right now. Today's Asia must be taken into consideration. In and through contemporary Asian realities the saving mission of Jesus will become more alive in Asia. This means attentiveness to the worlds of Asia.

The second thing that I discerned in terms of this appeal to be alert to the realities of Asia is this. I noticed in the Synod a deep sense of a celebration of the 'Asianess' of the Christian faith. I think the Holy Father was also behind this push. The Holy Father seldom talked and, in fact, did not intervene during the Synod's deliberations. He had the opening homily and the closing homily. Everyday he would have some remarks or short jokes to begin the session.

I remember one morning (I do not know whether he was joking but it had some punch to it) he said, "Jesus was born in Asia." I saw the bishops were very happy to be reminded that Jesus was born in Asia. Then the Pope added, "Oh! In that part of Asia that looked out to Europe." So, He was born on Asian soil but in that part of Asia that is open to the universal. He wanted to maintain the two dimensions. I noticed especially in the small group and in the Post-Synodal Council that there was this push to celebrate the *'Asianess'* of Christianity.

Jesus was born on Asian soil. He had within Him the cultural traditions of Asian people. That is why even in the way the Gospels were written and in the images employed, the methodology was very Asian in approach. The Church and the Christian movement, Christianity itself, all have Asian roots. That is what the Synod of Bishops wanted to bring to our attention as part of our missionary challenge. Can we celebrate the Asian aspect of the Christian faith? It was almost a refrain during the Synod that Christianity in Asia is still looked upon as something foreign, something alien. So, there is a need to recover the compatibility of the Christian faith with the Asian mentality, with the Asian cultures. In fact, the recovery of the Asian character of the saving Gospel is part of the missionary challenge of the Synod.

ADDITIONAL REFLECTION. Let me go to the third point. There was an awareness in the Synod that the unique contribution of Christians in Asia is our faith in Jesus Christ. We can collaborate with all other peoples of Asia in the quest for life, in the quest for justice, in the promotion of human dignity and all of those things. But the Synod also stressed the fact that what is unique to the Christian Churches is Jesus Christ. Nobody can share Jesus Christ the way we can. If there is anything that we can say to the people who are asking deep questions about life, our answer as Christians is Jesus and all that He stood for. That is our contribution.

In some quarters and small groups there was a reaction to some tendencies within theological and missiological circles to first bracket the faith element. One bishop from India depicted it this way; he said, "Many theologians and many missionaries will first somehow pretend that they are not Christians. They will bracket that fact in order to relate with others just on the human level. They say, 'we share a common humanity, so let the Christian element enter later on'." This bishop also said, "But the non-Christians are surprised that we are not mentioning Jesus, because if they know that you are a Christian, they expect you to talk about Jesus. So, why are you postponing that? Why are Christians hiding this fact while others are expecting it from you?" The discussion also went into pedagogy and methodology. The agreement and the consensus at the end of that session was: "Yes, we do not have to hide the truth that it is Jesus whom we are bringing to people. It is Jesus that we are proclaiming. In fact, that is our main contribution."

Now, this Christological focus is not as neat as it sounds. There are many complicated missionary and theological-pastoral issues connected with the proclamation of Jesus. One very important question raised in the Synod was: How do we understand Jesus as the Only Savior in the face of the many religions and soteriologies in Asia. That remains an issue. Another thing that surfaced was the meaning of Salvation. We say that Jesus came to bring salvation, but what is the meaning of salvation? How do you present it in a way that will make sense to the quest of Asian people for fuller life? What about the connection between Jesus and the Holy Spirit? Many bishops said that some people, in order to avoid talking about Jesus, just appeal to the Holy Spirit. But where you find the Spirit, there you find Jesus Christ. So, is there a need to mention Jesus Christ? In the Synod, there was a big push, especially from the bishops of India, to clarify the relationships between the Mission of Jesus and the Mission of the Spirit. They also asked more practical questions of how to present Jesus in ways appealing and understandable to Asians.

In addition, this question is not just in the area of theology, but also in terms of church, her structures and policies. Why? People will get to know the values of Jesus Christ through our policies, through our structures, through our ways of relating with one another in our communities. In fact, I remember one bishop even proposing that we in Asia should reflect on how the Papal Ministry should be conducted in a way that is in keeping with Asian mentalities. How do you rethink the Petrine Ministry in terms of Asian mentalities? This is not easy.

In the small group where I belonged there was a suggestion: "Maybe we should present Jesus as a Guru." Then, a bishop from China said, "People from China will not understand Guru. What is Guru? We will have to say: The Enlightened One. Jesus is the Enlightened One." In short, we must take images that are close to Asian mentalities and experiences and use them for the presentation of Jesus. That is my third point: the Christological focus and challenge of the Synod.

SPECIFIC MISSION CHALLENGES. Finally, the fourth area is more numerous and includes some specific areas of mission for the Church. In what areas of life in Asia did the Synod feel we should enter and bring the saving mission of Jesus? How do we incarnate the saving mission of Jesus? Here,

I identify five major areas which will probably appear in the Post-Synodal Exhortation, because these are some key areas raised by the bishops during the Synod.

The first specific item is the proclamation of Jesus. This has been the standing critique coming from the Vatican with regard to the documents from Asian bishops. They assert: We [Asians] are very weak in the proclamation of Jesus. Many of them fear that we are substituting dialogue for explicit proclamation of Jesus. So in the Synod this was affirmed vigorously: the need for explicit proclamation of Jesus. Of course, you know how the Asian bishops did it. They affirmed it, but then you look at the text of their interventions. What do the bishops of Asia understand by proclamation of Jesus? The first obvious thing is proclamation through the Word of God. In fact, some bishops were even proposing that biblical scholars in Asia start finding ways of doing exegesis in an Asian manner. Can Asian ways of interpreting texts evolve? They would be scientific but also attuned to the mentalities of Asian people.

Another bishop said, "The proclamation of Jesus must move through a contemplative life and an exchange among people (Catholics, Christians, non-Christians) in the area of contemplation." There was a strong reaction to the intervention of one bishop who said, "Why is it that in Asia, when people are looking for quality in education, in health care, social services, they instinctively go to Catholic institutions, Catholic hospitals, the Catholic Caritas and all of those things? But, when they are looking for spiritual guidance, they go to Buddhists, they go to Hindus."

Catholics in Asia are not known for their spiritual wisdom. So the Synod emphasized that the proclamation of the Word should be accompanied by a contemplative life. We have a long and rich contemplative tradition that can be part of the proclamation of Jesus. One bishop asserted that we have not maximized the contemplative tradition of the Church for missionary dialogue and the proclamation of Jesus. There is also proclamation through witness of life.

In short, the proclamation of Jesus was given prominence in the Synod, in the Post-Synodal Council's meetings, and in the recommendations to the Holy Father. The different Vatican offices and congregations were quite pleased. They are assured that the people in Asia believe in the proclamation of Jesus. They are really worried about that. I do not know why, but they are worried.

The second aspect or specific area of mission for the Church is Communion. *Communio* in the Church is a way of mission; communion is a way of missionary witness. The missionary proclamation is about Jesus, especially in Asia where there is always a search for harmony, harmony within human relationships and harmony with the cosmos. Therefore, if communities, especially Christian communities, could be witnesses to the possibility of communion, then we would be already proclaiming Jesus. The challenge is something *ad intra*, within the Church. The Church works for communion within itself as part of its missionary task. It is not simply an inward-looking thing; we settle our internal affairs so that we live in communion among ourselves. For the Synod, Communion is for Mission. So, communion in the BECs, communion in the parishes, communion in dioceses, and communion in the Universal Church is not just for smooth relationships within the Church, so that Christians will be in harmony with one another. It is part of our missionary proclamation.

Missionary proclamation in Asia, where harmony is given primary value, includes a particular calling here, in terms of communion. The communion with Churches in difficult situations is envisioned. The Holy Father mentioned it many times that when he wakes up in the morning, the first thing that he prays for is the Church in China. This intention also includes North Korea, but we are not even sure whether there is a Christian presence there. We have no news. Communion with people in difficult situations was a frequent Synod theme.

I was particularly moved by the interventions of the different bishops and administrators of the newly liberated republics in Central Asia, e.g. Kazakhstan, Kyrgizstan. The Archbishop of Iraq, a Chaldean, is the only bishop for the whole of Iraq, for all the Chaldeans. He has only sixty priests for the whole country. He asked me, "How many priests are there in your diocese?" I said, "We are close to eighty." He said, "Look at that; that is only one diocese, and we have the whole country with only sixty. Send some of them to us." I said, "Yes, we will send." I said yes, but I do not know whom to send!

Then he said another thing, "Please help us reflect on the mystery of the disappearance of the primitive Churches. Many of these Churches were even founded by the Apostles. But it is a mystery to us. Why does the Lord allow these Churches to disappear?" Then he said, "Are we not to be true to our vocation in Asia? Are we not being called, really, to be the little flock? Should we really work towards increasing numbers of Christians? Or, is it our calling in Asia to disappear?" This is a very difficult missionary question.

I was surprised that when he talked about the mystery of the disappearance of the primitive Churches he said, "Should we go against the calling? Is it a calling? Can we really be called to remain a little flock? Should I not be faithful to that? Is it part of the missionary challenge of the Church in Asia, not to increase, but maybe even to disappear. And when that moment comes, not to resist it." I told him, "Bishop, I am not prepared to answer. That is a difficult question."

The third specific area is Dialogue. This is not new to us anymore. For the past twenty-seven years or so, the basic intuition of the FABC is that the mode of mission for Asia, the mode of evangelization for Asia, is dialogue. What is new is that this was elevated to the universal level during the Synod; I believe it has been sanctioned. I believe the mission of dialogue will be part of the Apostolic Exhortation. So, although there is nothing new, we are very happy that what some used to fear, dialogue, will now even be proposed. Of course, we will wait, because at this time we do not have the final Apostolic Exhortation.

Another specific area for mission focuses on peace-making. It was Bishop Hamao from Japan who really pushed for this, as one of the areas where Jesus' mission of love, service and life be intensified in Asia. I thought it was good that it came from him; his intervention was almost like a public confession. He went back to World War II; he recalled some of the unjust things that were done by the Japanese forces during that time. He said that the Church in Japan did not raise its voice against all those inhumanities. He also said that we really have to commit ourselves to the promotion of peace. It was a wonderful occasion. I felt some sort of healing, forgiveness and reconciliation.

Finally, another specific area of mission for Asia is developing, forming, and preparing agents for mission, agents of the Gospel of Life. Here the basic intuition of the FABC was again affirmed. Of course, the Holy Spirit is the principal agent of mission, but in Asia it is the local Churches that are really the missionary agents—not individuals but local Churches. All the different sectors that comprise the local Church are to be animated for mission. There was even a suggestion that tourists and overseas workers could be tapped for evangelizing work. All sectors means people who work in social communication, women, families, the youth, laity, religious, communities of apostolic life and different pastors.

CONCLUSION. As you see, some of these things are not new. We are already aware of these different areas. We should not take these areas in isolation from what we have already mentioned regarding the mission of Jesus Christ, regarding the Asian realities and the awareness that our unique contribution to mission in Asia is our faith in Jesus Christ. I cannot go through all the Synod details here. I am not even sure how the Holy Father will discuss these elements in the Apostolic Exhortation.

I have a concluding remark. The fruits of the Synod will be shared with us in November here in Asia. Before the opening of the Church's celebrations of the great jubilee of redemption, I think it is appropriate that the fruits and theme of the Synod will be shared with all of us here in Asia. The focus will be on Jesus the Redeemer. So, the Church in Asia will face the new millennium with her eyes focused on Jesus the Redeemer, Jesus the Only Savior.

I think the Post-Synodal reflection will alert us to the fact that Jesus is not only the message to be proclaimed in our missionary work. Jesus is the Missioner who should not be replaced. He will remain the Missionary here in Asia. So, He is both the Message and the Agent. He is the Message to be proclaimed; He is the Missioner that must do the work. I think one fundamental challenge for the Churches of Asia is to take that seriously. If Jesus is not the Message, if Jesus is not both the Message and the Missioner for us, then we might be betraying His being the Savior. For Him to be the Only Savior means He is not only the Message but also the one who will do His Mission.

Ours is a modest contribution. We are not substituting for Jesus. We are not substituting for His Spirit. We are to be more of a discerning Church, waiting for the Lord to indicate to us where we will cast our nets. But, He must direct the catch, because He is the One who is Missioner. I do not always know how to translate that into concrete areas of mission. However, I think underneath all of these areas of mission which the Holy Father will propose to us for scrutiny in his Apostolic Exhortation, there is a fundamental challenge. We are to become more spiritual. We must adjust our missionary perspective: Jesus is the missioner, and we are just participating in His mission.

Father Luis Antonio "Chito" Tagle, a priest from the Diocese of Imus, Philippines, completed his theological and graduate studies at the Loyola School of Theology in Manila and at the Catholic University of America in Washington. His numerous apostolic commitments include: rector of the Tahanan ng Mabuting Pastol, pastor of the Cathedral in Imus, professor at several schools of theology, and member of the International Theological Commission.

Chapter 7

THE SOUL OF MISSION

Gaudencio B. Rosales, D.D.

THE MISSION OF LOVE AND SERVICE IN ASIA. Evangelization is not only a task for the Church. It is its life. The Vatican II Decree *Ad Gentes* reiterates that mission itself is to bring the Good News and is the very nature of the Church, following the plan of the Father and receiving its origin from the mission of the Son and the Holy Spirit (AG 2). Thus it is necessary that the Church understands what it is being sent for and what it is supposed to proclaim.

The Synod of Bishops for Asia convened with His Holiness, Pope John Paul II, and discussed the theme: *Jesus Christ the Savior and His Mission of Love and Service in Asia:* "... *That They May have Life, and have it Abundantly*" (John 10:10). The Asian Synod participates in the Continental Synodal Assemblies as part of the preparation for the Great Jubilee of 2000.

Similar to all the Synods, the Synod for Asia followed the usual Synodal procedure: (1) preparation through consultation with episcopal conferences through a series of questions in the *Lineamenta*; (2) the publication of the

Instrumentum Laboris, which is the main guide to discussion; it clusters ideas and themes; (3) the interventions on the Synod floor; (4) group discussions; (5) reports before and after the discussions; (6) the presentation of propositions; (7) approval of propositions; (8) the Message of the Asian Synod.

The Final Message of the Synodal Fathers is still part of the Synod. The only official document, like in any past Synods, will be the Apostolic Exhortation that the Holy Father will issue a year or so after the closing of that Assembly of Shepherds from Asia.

THE GRAVE REALITIES OF ASIA. No one talks about this continent without bringing in the question of numbers. Asia makes up more than half of the planet's population. China and India today account for more than a third of the world's people. Some of the world's poorest people struggle to live in Asia. The freest economic market encouraged by the West can also be found in this continent. Almost all of Asia's countries in the past have been colonies of the West and sometimes by Asians themselves. The longest living traditions and some of the world's oldest cultures as well as all the world's five great old religions—Hinduism, Buddhism, Judaism, Christianity and Islam—were born in Asia.

With the exception of the Philippines, Christians are a very small minority in Asia. Just looking at the demographic panorama will convince anyone that the greater mission for the Church awaits her right here in the vast continent of Asia.

THE MISSION OF THE CHURCH. The mission of the Church is to proclaim Jesus Christ as the Son of the Father. In and through Him the Father is known and communicates Himself. Jesus is the messenger and message of Life (Jn 6:68). There is no way of interpreting his message and actions as mere personal deportment with social upliftment consequences. Jesus preaches the Father's Kingdom and witnesses in life and in death to its values of Justice, Peace and Love.

This Jesus of God's love (Jn 3:16) must be proclaimed both in word and in life. Proclamation by word! Pope Paul VI in the Apostolic Exhortation, *Evangelii Nuntiandi* (42), reminds us that "the word remains ever relevant, especially when it is the bearer of the power of God. And for this reason, St. Paul's axiom 'Faith comes from what is heard' (Rm 10:17) also retains its relevance."

This Jesus, who is our salvation, remains to be proclaimed. It was through his death, the breaking of his body and shedding of his blood, that we receive the forgiveness of sins. His death is the expression of the greatest love of God for us. This love expressed by and in Jesus is what we proclaim.

There is no silencing of Christians in mission. They preach Jesus and are on the alert to catch many occasions to mention Him and His message in the milieu where they are. As a well known communicator once said: the evangelizer takes every opportunity to bring Jesus in public interviews and media exposure.

The uniqueness which is Asia—brought up and bred within its own millennia of rich traditions, cultures and ancient religions—carries the challenge to the Church of presenting Christ with "an Asian face," using Asian concepts, terms and cultures. Very probably a poor Christ rather than a rich, powerful one is more readily understood by large Asian masses who wallow in poverty.

What really will make Christ acceptable to the Asian? Listening to proclamation becomes more compelling when the message reechoes in life. "Modern man listens more willingly to witnesses than to teachers, and if he does listen to teachers, it is because they are witnesses" (EN 41). These days there is a glut of talk, words, speeches, lectures, conferences, conventions, and assemblies. Speech and word have been overworked. We need "word-processors"! How much of this actually translates into conviction or converts to action, and then settles finally into the behavior of Christians?

"Let your light [life] shine in the sight of men, so that, seeing your good works, they may give the praise to your Father in heaven" (Mt 5:16). He is the true light that enlightens all people. Jesus is the Word and Light of God (Jn 1:9). He is proclaimed also in word and in life. The world awaits examples and witnesses.

PROCLAIMER 'TO' OR 'WITH' THE PROCLAIMED? A DIALOGUE. The proclaimer is at home with people. Jesus was sought by people: "Everybody is looking for you." He was also attracted to more people: "Let us go elsewhere, to the neighboring towns, so that I can preach there too, because that is why I came" (Mk 1:37-38). This is the Christ that is presented to people; he is a person who is a friend of all. The proclaimer is a person in dialogue.

Dialogue with poverty is for Jesus mutual communing with people who are poor like him. The proclaimer here seeks equal status with persons to whom he brings the proclamation. The approach is never done from the post of superiority. The first step for the proclaimer in dialogue is humility.

The Asian proclaimer is ever reminded that the task of evangelization for the Church in Asia calls for the triple dialogue with people, cultures and religions; this was officially declared in the Final Statement of FABC I, *Evangelization in Modern Day Asia,* held in Taipei in 1974.

A special training to sensitivity and respect is a required of a proclaimer in Asia. This is so not only because Asia puts high value and respect on persons, particularly its elders, but also because of the wealth and reverence their ancient religions and traditions have accumulated through their own millennia.

In *Ad Gentes* Vatican II expresses the same reverence in this way: "They [Christians and all proclaimers] should be familiar with their national and religious traditions and uncover with gladness and respect those seeds of the Word which lie hidden in them.... Just as Christ penetrated to the hearts of men and by a truly human dialogue led them to the divine light, so too his disciples, profoundly pervaded by the Spirit of Christ, should know and converse with those among whom they live, that through sincere and patient dialogue these men might learn of the riches which a generous God has distributed among the nations" (AG 11).

DIALOGUE WITH CREATION. If only the awareness of ecological imbalance brought about by an abuse in human consumption and carelessness had come earlier, the dialogue with creation should have been included in the FABC I Taipei Declaration of 1974. However, world consciousness of the need to protect the integrity of creation came very, very late. The universal declaration of an emergency state for world resources—such as its disappearing tropical forests, denudation of mountains, erosion and desertification, waste mismanagement, pollution of sea bodies, water loss in aquifers ushering in the age of bottled water, air pollution, noise pollution, ozone layer destruction—came only through the Earth Summit in Rio de Janeiro, June 1992. The key word for the Rio de Janeiro Earth Summit was "Sustainable Development"!

Can we still escape an Ecological Armageddon? The *Catechism of the Catholic Church* states briefly but with urgency the need to respect and protect the integrity of creation when it placed the mandate under the Seventh Commandment: "Thou Shalt Not Steal." The implication is that if an individual abuses creation's resources or its modification, he or she is stealing from the future generations. "The Seventh Commandment enjoins respect for the integrity of creation. Animals, like plants and inanimate beings, are by nature destined for the common good of the past, present and future humanity.... Man's dominion over inanimate and other living beings granted by the Creator is not absolute; it is limited by concern for the quality of life of his neighbor, including generations to come; it requires a religious respect for the integrity of creation" (CCC, 2415).

For the Catholic Catechism the key word is "Stewardship." The concern and respect for the integrity of creation is both part of the Christian Catechism and Spirituality!

THE SOUL OF MISSION: THE SPIRITUALITY OF THE PROCLAIMER. No proclamation, no evangelization, is possible without the Holy Spirit. Jesus was no exception; this is clear as He stood up to read in the Synagogue one day: "The Spirit of the Lord has been given to me, for he has anointed me...to bring the good news to the poor, to proclaim liberty to captives, sight to the blind, to set the downtrodden free and to proclaim the Lord's year of favor" (Lk 4:17-19).

By himself the proclaimer causes little or no ripple in the heart of listeners. "The Holy Spirit is the principal agent of evangelization; it is he who impels each individual to proclaim the Gospel, and it is he who in the depths of consciences causes the word of salvation to be accepted and understood" (EN 75). Thus, the proclaimer begins his preparation with a special devotion to the Holy Spirit, making Him a part of his prayer and devotion, always befriending Him and His inspiration in daily life.

The spirituality of the proclaimer is rooted in the person of Jesus whom he/she intimately approaches through prayer, reading the Word and reflection. The Evangelizer is an active apostle, ministering to people through the dialogues described earlier, but he also is a contemplative in between the ministries. The proclaimer is a prayerful person.

To lead others to pray, the proclaimer must himself be deeply steeped in prayer, its practice and spirit. In Asia, a guru is not just a teacher nor a leader. He is a man who prays and who lives the very teachings he imparts. Most importantly, a guru is a man of goodness.

A PERSON OF COMPASSION. Asians listen to persons and not precisely to the intricacies of the doctrinal teaching. This is true especially of the simple and poor people. And, of the many possible people to listen to, the crowd watches for the compassionate person, the one who knows pity and sympathy. A good man stands out as a merciful one; he is never hidden in a crowd.

The Jesus whom we proclaim is one such person. He saw a large crowd on the shore as He stepped out of the boat and He "took pity on them because they were like sheep without a shepherd" (Mk 6:34). And, people were attracted to Him.

Thus, the Christian proclaimer in Asia must be prepared for a ministry and life of compassion. It must be more than a matter of practice and prayer. Compassion should, in the end, become part of his life, its many expressions and constant reaching out to people. Mercy shown to even a hidden beggar has a way of reflecting itself to the world, even if only through a silent smile. Compassion transcends barriers of any kind. No wonder, Jesus used it for disarming even hardened men and known sinners: "Neither do I condemn you; go home, and do not sin anymore" (Jn 8:11).

As the writer Christian Bovee puts it: "Kindness and compassion is a language the dumb can speak and deaf can hear."

SPIRITUAL GUIDES AND NOT SIMPLY EFFICIENT ADMINISTRATORS. Time and again the hunger for spiritual guides was raised at the Asian Bishops' Synod General Assembly in the presence of the Holy Father; it continued reverberating in different small workshops and discussions. There was no mistaking that one was in Asia, when the desire for spiritual guides kept coming back, because a "guru" in Hinduism is a personal spiritual teacher and guide.

It came as no surprise that it was the Synod for Asian Bishops that asked for spiritual guides and teachers. "Christians in Asia need more zealous pastors and spiritual guides and not simply efficient administrators" (Message of the Asian Synod, No. 5).

The proclaimers in Asia are to be trained above all as spiritual guides, pastors and lastly as administrators. The Asian ideal of teacher and guide (in the guru system) is really akin to a personal tutorial method of instruction. It is a personal transmission from guru to student / devotee. It is the same method as the Master to Disciples / Apostles method. It is the "Jesus-to-His-Apostles" method.

The need for the proclaimer—through formation—to first imbibe the doctrine and live the Truth before it is shared with the disciples is evident in Vatican II's Decree on Priestly Formation when it said, "They [the proclaimers, the priests] should live His Paschal Mystery in such a way that they will know how to initiate into it the people committed to their care" (OT 8).

For the proclaimer in Asia, the grave message from the Synod of Asian Bishops is this: Imbibe (through study and prayer) the Mystery of Jesus, Son of the Father, Our Life and Savior, before proclaiming Him to others (through word and witness of life). Then only will Christ live in others, because He has first found life in the proclaimer.

Gaudencio B. Rosales, D.D., current Archbishop of Lipa, is known as a "mission advocate" and "friend of missionaries" in the Philippines. He has made significant contributions in various positions: National Director of the Pontifical Mission Aid Societies, Overall Director of the 1979 International Congress on Mission in Manila, and Advisor to the Philippine Mission Society.

CHAPTER **8**

PROMOTING AN ASIAN MISSIONARY RESPONSE

On April 24, 1998 during the Ninth General Congregation of the Special Assembly for Asia of the Synod of Bishops, Father Edward F. Malone, M.M., Assistant Secretary General of the Federation of Asian Bishops' Conferences (FABC), addressed the assembly. His intervention focused on the emergence of missionary commitment within Asia and on the Asian-born Missionary Societies of Apostolic Life. A summary of Malone's intervention follows:

1. Asian Christians and local Churches have a deep sense of gratitude for the gift of faith they have received from God, and as the fruit of the dedicated labor and sacrifice of missionaries.

2. Although the number of Christians remains small in comparison with Asia's burgeoning masses (two to three percent of all Asian peoples), this "little flock" (Lk 12:32) seeks to share its riches and discovery of Christ with neighboring peoples.

3. The challenge to proclaim the Gospel in Asia is great.

4. Most international missionary institutes have a home in Asia. I wish to highlight a unique and essential form of missionary response—missionary society of apostolic life.

5. Six such societies of men have emerged in Asia: the Missionary Society of the Philippines; the Missionary Society of St. Thomas the Apostle (India); the Catholic Foreign Mission Society of Korea; the Missionary Society of Thailand; the Lorenzo Ruiz Mission Society (Philippines); and, the Heralds of Good News (India).

6. Their contribution is: *ad gentes, ad exteros,* and *ad vitam.*

7. With the renewal of ecclesiology, a wide variety of mission initiatives must necessarily emerge from within each local Church.

8. The number of societies of apostolic life which are working in Asia is large. Now it is Asia's turn to give, to be a continent of missionary hope.

9. Missionary societies can become "bridges of communion." The contribution of missionary societies of apostolic life are: Asians evangelizing Asians; the emergence of missionary local Churches; the strengthening of bonds of communion among the Churches of Asia and of "communion and filial oneness with the See of Peter."

Some developments that foster (or hinder) mission:

1. The missionaries foster communion among Sister Churches.

2. Churches that do not experience sending / receiving become closed in upon themselves.

3. If the mission *ad gentes* is not promoted, there will remain many unreached peoples.

4. Pastoral care is not to derail the local Church mission effort.

5. The actual foundation of Asian-born missionary societies is to be fostered in each local Church.

NOTE: The foregoing summary appeared in L'*Osservatore Romano* (English Edition) on May 13, 1998, page 14.

* * * * * * * * * * * * * * *

In light of the Malone intervention, a specific recommendation appeared as "Proposition 28" in the final 59 propositions sent to the Holy Father for his consideration in composing the post-synodal apostolic exhortation. The text of the specific proposition follows:

MISSIONARY SOCIETIES OF APOSTOLIC LIFE
AND OTHER MISSIONARY SOCIETIES

Missionary institutes of apostolic life and other Missionary Societies continue to render a great service to the cause of evangelization in Asia [as they have done] during the past. Their contribution is gratefully acknowledged and desired to be continued now and in the future. This will favor a further growth of the missionary institutes of apostolic life, which recently have been founded in several countries of Asia, as the expression of the missionary dimension and responsibility of the Churches in Asia for the evangelization of their own continent and of the whole world.

This Synod recommends the establishment within each local Church of Asia, where such do not exist, of missionary societies of apostolic life, characterized by their commitment exclusively for the mission *ad gentes*, *ad exteros* and *ad vitam*.

Part Three

ASIAN REALITIES AND PERSPECTIVES

CHAPTER 9

CHALLENGING ASIAN MISSION STATISTICS

The challenge of being a missionary church in Asia can effectively be highlighted by understanding important demographical realities obtaining throughout the continent. Current Asian statistics may surprise and often startle; they can shake our complacency; they concretize the task at hand: *mission and evangelization in modern day Asia.*

Asia, the world's largest and most populated continent, constitutes one third of the land area of the whole world (17,124,000 square miles) and is home to almost 60% of humanity. It is a continent of the young (about 40% are below 15 years of age); there are more than 30 mega-cities in Asia with populations ranging from 5 to 20 million. The nine most populous nations (in descending order) are: China, India, Indonesia, Japan, Bangladesh, Pakistan, Vietnam, Philippines, and Thailand. China's population exceeds one billion; India's populace is predicted to cross the one billion mark in the year 2000. With this massive bulk goes a wide variety of diversity and contrasts—physical, ethnic, social, economic, political, religious.

As Cardinal Stephen Kim Sou-hwan of Korea noted at the Asian Synod in Rome (April 18 - May 14, 1998), Asia is not only made up of "various nations, but, one might say, many worlds." Thus, there are in a sense many Asias. It is a conglomerate of "continents" and giant archipelagoes; it has a rich mosaic of cultures and sub-cultures; it also has a wealth of spiritual heritages. In a word, any attempt to weld this diversity together will sacrifice some detail and result in generalizations. Although they reflect accuracy, statistics have their limitations.

Asia is a continent rich in non-Christian cultures. It is the homeland of three eminent world religions: Hinduism, Buddhism, and Islam; 85% of all the world's non-Christians are in Asia and they adhere to several of the great religions. Hinduism, born about 5,000 years ago, has about 650 million followers, most of them in India and neighboring countries. Buddhism is a religion and philosophy developed from Hinduism by Siddhartha Gautama, (the "Enlightened One"); it has 300 million followers, mostly in Asia.

Islam, established by Muhammad in the seventh century, is a monotheistic religion; it incorporates elements of Judaic and Christian belief. Islam numbers some 700 million followers in Asia alone; the Catholics of Asia are slightly over 100 million. The two largest Islamic nations in the world are found in Asia: Indonesia and Bangladesh—each have well over 100 million Muslims. Other significant religious and philosophical-ethical systems in Asia are Confucianism, Taoism, Shintoism, as well as many indigenous, traditional belief systems.

THE CATHOLIC CHURCH IN ASIA. Catholics world-wide constitute 17.2% of all people; all Christians are 33.1% of humanity. In Asia, Catholics (105.2 million in 1997) represent only 2.9% of the nearly 3.5 billion Asians. Significantly, well over 50% of all Asian Catholics are found in one country alone—the Philippines. Thus, if one excludes the Philippines, Asia is only about one percent

Catholic; this leaves very small minorities of Catholics in most Asian nations.

The Church in Asia continues to grow. In 1988 there were 84.3 million Catholics; by 1997 they had reached 105.2 million (an increase of 20.9 million or 25%). The number of priests rose from 27,700 to 32,291 during the 1988-1997 nine-year period. Asian seminarians increased from 19,090 to 25,842 in this same period. Asian countries with the most seminarians (given in descending order) are: India, Philippines, South Korea, and Vietnam. In 1997 Asia had 617 out of the 4,420 bishops in the world.

The 1997 statistic of 32,291 priests in Asia includes 17,789 diocesan priests and 14,502 religious priests. Two-thirds of all religious priests are Asians; the vast majority (86%) of religious sisters are also Asian. The countries with the largest number of indigenous sisters (in descending rank) are: India, Philippines, South Korea, Japan, Indonesia, and Vietnam.

The Church in Asia is known for its commitment to education. 1998 statistics present the following data: kindergartens (9,388) with 1,861,530 students; elementary/primary schools (13,467) with 4,660,914 students; secondary schools (7,935) with 4,195,208 students; the number of students in Catholic higher institutes is 703,834.

An interesting exercise is to shrink the entire earth's population into a village of precisely 100 people, with all the existing human ratios remaining the same. In this village there would be 57 Asians, 21 Europeans, 14 from the Western Hemisphere, both north and south, and 8 Africans. Of these 100 persons 52 would be female and 48 would be male. There would be 70 people of color and 30 would be white. Religiously, 67 would be non-Christian and 33 would be Christians. Out of 100 people 70 would be unable to read; 50 would suffer from malnutrition; 1 would be near death; 1

would be near birth; 1 (only 1) would have a college education; and, 1 would own a computer.

INDIVIDUAL COUNTRY STATISTICS. This presentation now turns its focus to individual Asian nations in the FABC Region of Asia. Abundant statistics are available; only two items will be included. For each FABC country the estimated population in millions for the year 2000 is listed; this is followed by the percentage of Catholics in that nation.

Bangladesh (145.8m / 0.27%);   **Bhutan** (1.8m / 0.02%); **Burma/Myanmar** (48.8m / 1.3%);   **Cambodia** (10.3m / 0.02%); **China** (1,239.5m / 0.5%);   **Hong Kong** (6.9m / 4.7%);   **India** (990m / 1.72%);   **Indonesia** (202m / 2.58%);   **Japan** (127.7m / 0.36%);   **Korea-North** (22.6m / ?);   **Korea-South** (47.2m / 6.7%); **Laos** (6.2m / 0.9%);   **Macau** (0.5m / 5%);   **Malaysia** (22m / 3%); **Mongolia** (2.5m / ?);   **Nepal** (23m / 0.05%);   **Pakistan** (142.6m / 0.6%);   **Philippines** (74.8m / 81%);   **Singapore** (3.1m / 6.5%); **Sri Lanka** (20.8m / 8%);   **Taiwan** (22.1m / 1.4%);   **Thailand** (61.6m / 0.4%);   **Vietnam** (78.2m / 6.1%).

CONCLUDING REFLECTIONS. These few secular and religious statistics already indicate that "being a missionary church in Asia" demands creative, innovative, dialogical and inculturated approaches to Gospel proclamation. In addition, although beyond the scope of this short presentation, one should also consider diverse cultural, political, social and economic realities in envisioning a pastoral program of integral evangelization. The task before the local churches is great; they must respond with enthusiasm and insight!

Though numerically small, the churches of Asia are a blessed and vigorous minority. This fact was clearly recognized during the Asian Synod; some of its words in the *Final Message* (nos. 7-8) can be a source of genuine optimism for Asia's local churches. Why? "Our greatest reason for hope is Jesus Christ, who said: 'Take heart, it is I;

have no fear' (Mt 14:27), and 'I have overcome the world' (Jn 16:33)." "So let us be confident. The Spirit of the Lord is obviously at work in Asia, and the church is quite active in this continent." "This is the work of the Holy Spirit, who is always the one at our side to help us."

NOTE: For continuous sources of updated religious statistics, three reference works are recommended: *Catholic Almanac* (Our Sunday Visitor, Inc.), *Statistical Yearbook of the Church* (Vatican Press), and "Annual Statistical Table on Global Mission" in the first number of each volume of *International Bulletin of Missionary Research*.

CHAPTER 10

ASIA'S EMERGING CATHOLICITY

FABC INSIGHTS ON THE LOCAL CHURCH

Explore any major document that has emerged from the reflection of the Federation of Asian Bishops' Conferences (FABC) during its quarter-century existence and you will find creative insights on the Local Church in the Asian context. Historically, it was the 1970 Asian pastoral visit of Pope Paul VI that gave the impetus for the local churches to begin formulating a vision of church and mission adequate to the "new world being born" in Asia in the post-colonial period. They asked themselves: How would local faith-communities respond to "the grace that was the Second Vatican Council"? How would the churches incarnate a decisive "turning to history" and a "turning to the Gospel" within history "for all the peoples of Asia"? [1]

Consistent, prolonged, pastoral and theological reflection on the Church and her mission of evangelization has enabled the FABC to articulate an overall vision that captures what "being Church in Asia today" truly means. The insights have grown out of a belief that the Spirit was "speaking to the churches." Without doubt, many creative FABC ecclesiological insights center on the meaning, theology, and lived experience of local church.

FABC pastoral-theological reflection is decidedly inductive—emerging from life's concrete realities. Therefore, an ecclesiology with local church as its focal point most adequately captures the hopes and aspirations of local peoples. As the community of Jesus' disciples in Asia, the Church consistently links her identity with Asia's peoples and their life situations. She seeks to be—in fact, not only in theory—the "Church of the poor" and the "Church of the young." She shares the vicissitudes of the "Church of silence" in several parts of Asia. Her pastoral priorities concern the displaced (refugees and migrants), women and the girl-child, youth, families, the poor, the followers of Asia's great religious traditions. She actively fosters increasing communion among local Asian churches in filial oneness with the See of Peter, which presides over the universal Church in love; she promotes authentic catholicity.

In a word, the theological thematic of LOCAL CHURCH provides an appropriate, integrating center for the life of Asia's faith-communities. This fact helps explain why internationally some of the very best theological reflection on local church has emerged in Asia and through the FABC. **[2]** Telling the story of local church in Asian/FABC theological reflection—with all its depth, richness, and inspiration—is the central focus of this modest presentation. **[3]**

FABC I. The first FABC plenary assembly was held in Taipei, Taiwan in April 1974; it focused on the theme: "Evangelization in Modern Day Asia" (it was also a preparation for the Synod on Evangelization to be held in Rome later that same year). The Asian churches through their bishops defined the central and most urgent mission duty incumbent upon them:

"The primary focus of our task of evangelization then, at this time in our history, is the building up of a truly local church. For the local church is the realization and the enfleshment of the Body of Christ in a given people, a given place and time" (FABC I, 9-10).

"It is not a community in isolation from other communities of the Church one and catholic. Rather it seeks communion with all of them. With them it professes the one faith, shares the one Spirit and the one sacramental life. In a special way it rejoices in its communion and filial oneness with the See of Peter, which presides over the universal Church in love" (FABC I, 11).

"The local church is a church incarnate in a people, a church indigenous and inculturated. And this means concretely a church in continuous, humble and loving dialogue with the living traditions, the cultures, the religions—in brief, with all the life-realities of the people in whose midst it has sunk its roots deeply and whose history and life it gladly makes its own. It seeks to share in whatever truly belongs to that people: its meanings and its values, its aspirations, its thoughts and its language, its songs and its artistry. Even its frailties and failings it assumes, so that they too may be healed. For so did God's Son assume the totality of our fallen human condition (save only for sin) so that He might make it truly His own, and redeem it in His paschal mystery" (FABC I, 12).

ASIAN COLLOQUIUM ON MINISTRIES IN THE CHURCH. Three years later in 1977, during the Asian Colloquium on Ministries in the Church (ACMC) held in Hong Kong, the theme of local church received another impetus:

"...the decisive new phenomenon for Christianity in Asia will be the emergence of genuine Christian communities in Asia—Asian in their way of thinking, praying, living, communicating their own Christ-experience to others. The consequences will be tremendous not only for the ministries the Asian Churches will have to perform but also for all aspects of their life. We should beware of seeing our future mission in categories that belong to the past, when the West shaped the Churches' history. If the Asian Churches do not discover their own identity, they will have no future" (ACMC 14).

"Each local Church is determined by her human context and lives in a dialectical relationship with the human society into which she is inserted as the Gospel leaven.... Each local Church, in order to be viable, needs to become fully responsible and must have the legitimate autonomy which her natural and harmonious growth demands" (ACMC 25).

"Asian Churches then must become truly Asian in all things. The principle of indigenization and inculturation is at the very root of their coming into their own. The ministry of Asian Churches, if it is to be authentic, must be relevant to Asian societies. This calls on the part of the Churches for originality, creativity and inventiveness, for boldness and courage" (ACMC 26).

"Since Christ's mission is universal, all local Churches are called to live in communion with each other. This bond of unity, visibly expressed in the college of bishops presided over by the Bishop of Rome, implies that the search of each Church for ministries adapted to her needs is subject to verification and testing by the other Churches. In this bond of union lies the guarantee of the true apostolicity and catholicity of each local Church" (ACMC 27).

FABC II. The Second FABC Plenary Assembly (Calcutta, 1978) was organized around the theme: "Prayer—The Life of the Church of Asia." The Bishops-delegate noted that an important motive for their assembly was "to deepen our knowledge of our local churches" (FABC II, 1), and they addressed "the tasks which the carrying-out of the mission of the Church in Asia demands: commitment to the upbuilding of Asian communities in the life of the Gospel, to inculturation of Christian faith and life, to the endeavor for total human development and authentic liberation of peoples in justice and love, to interreligious dialogue and to renewed missionary formation" (FABC II, 3).

INTERNATIONAL MISSION CONGRESS. The successful International (though predominantly Asian) Congress on Mission (IMC) held in 1979 in Manila once again strongly affirmed the centrality of the local church for a "new age of mission" in Asia.

"What is the newness of this 'new age of mission'? First, the realization in practice that 'mission' is no longer, and can no longer be, a one-way movement from the 'older churches' to the 'younger churches,' from the churches of the old Christendom to the churches in the colonial lands. Now—as Vatican II already affirmed with all clarity and force—every local church is and cannot be but missionary. Every local church is 'sent' by Christ and the Father to bring the Gospel to its surrounding milieu, and to bear it also into all the world. For every local church this is a *primary* task. Hence we are moving beyond both the vocabulary and the idea of 'sending churches' and 'receiving churches,' for as living communities of the one Church of Jesus Christ, every local church must be a sending church, and every local church (because it is not on earth ever a total realization of the Church) must also be a receiving church. Every local church is responsible for its mission, and co-responsible for the mission of all its sister-churches. Every local church, according to its possibilities, must share whatever its gifts are, for the needs of other churches, for mission throughout [hu]mankind, for the life of the world" (IMC 14).

"Once again, what is the newness of this 'new age of mission'? We believe that the Spirit of the Lord calls each people and each culture to its own fresh and creative response to the Gospel. Each local church has its own vocation in the one history of salvation, in the one Church of Christ. In each local church, each people's history, each people's culture, meanings and values, each people's traditions are taken up, not diminished nor destroyed, but celebrated and renewed, purified if need be, and fulfilled (as the Second Vatican Council teaches) in the life of the Spirit" (IMC 15).

Two workshop papers (V and VII) of the Manila Mission Congress spoke eloquently of the local church. The participants of Workshop VII noted: "We recognize that the local church is the center and source of evangelization" (1). "Just as it is the responsibility of the Christian to work for the growth and development of the local church, in the same way he must become aware of his responsibility toward churches in other parts of the world" (9). This means that "Each local church is co-responsible with its sister churches everywhere, Rome being the foundation and center, for the building up of the kingdom of God throughout the world" (9).

The same document affirms that "Missionaries from sister churches are not only living signs of the universality of the Church and the existence of co-responsibility, but because of their different cultural and Christian background, they enrich and fruitfully challenge the local church.

The local church should welcome, accept and help integrate them into its life" (10).

FABC III. The Third FABC Plenary Assembly (Bangkok, 1982) chose "The Church—A Community of Faith in Asia" as its central theme. Again, one finds enlightening words on the local church; the final statement noted:

"We have seen...how the local church must be a community of graced communion rooted in the life of the Trinity, a community of prayer and contemplation, and of sacramental celebration and life centered around the Eucharist. It must be defined by its life of faithful discipleship in the Gospel, patterned on the Paschal Mystery of Jesus, 'a community for others.' We have realized that genuine participation and co-responsibility must be essential elements of its existence, and theological reflection and discernment integral components of its life. It is a community which strives to remain in unfeigned unity with its pastors, within the bonds of local and universal communion in the one Church" (FABC III, 15).

THESES ON THE LOCAL CHURCH. The centrality of the local church in the theological-missiological thought in the Asian area is highlighted by the FABC commitment to study the question in depth. The FABC has promoted indigenous Asian theological reflection since its early years; the formal establishment of the Theological Advisory Commission (TAC) of the FABC came in the 1980s. A five-year period of extensive study and consultation culminated in a comprehensive document entitled "Theses on the Local Church: A Theological Reflection in the Asian Context" (TLC). This is one of the longest documents ever produced by the TAC (well over 50 closely printed pages); it was released in January 1991. In the opinion of this author, worldwide it is probably the best and most comprehensive document to date on "local church."

The FABC-TAC document on the local church contains several sections. After a lengthy contextualized introduction and clarification of terms, the fifteen theses are presented in two thematic sections: "Biblical Foundations" (Theses 1-4) and "The Birth, Life and Mission of the Local Church" (Theses 5-15). Next, a concluding section follows; finally, a wide variety of practical "Pastoral Corollaries and Recommendations" are presented. Some salient quotes serve to capture the spirit of this insightful piece of Asian theological reflection on the local church:

"Already, as we have noted, the First Plenary Assembly of the FABC spoke of building up of the local Church as the present focus of the Church's mission in Asia. That discernment remains valid today [1991].... More and more the local Churches in Asia must see themselves as responsible agents for the self-realization of the Church" (TLC: C, 3-4).

"We see the emergence of the world of the Third Millennium already upon us.... Whether the Gospel shall be present in this new age with its unpredictable turnings and its manifold diversity will depend greatly on whether local Churches fulfill their vocation in the historic moment which is now upon them. We grasp something of the significance of local Church and inculturation in this context; those who cannot understand this fail to resonate with the signs of our time, and the heartbeat of our peoples" (TLC: C, 5).

"We must surely be grateful that we experience today the 'rush of the Spirit' in our Churches. For it is a privileged moment for local theological reflection and discernment, for the gathering and spending of energies, for the upbuilding of authentic local Churches in our part of the world.... We can only pray that we may listen and be obedient to the Spirit, that we may be guided by his creative power and be filled by the commitment and courage which are his gifts" (TLC: C, 6-7).

FABC V. Most major documents of the FABC refer explicitly to the role of the local church in mission and evangelization. The Fifth Plenary FABC Assembly held in Bandung, Indonesia (July 1990), with the theme "Journeying Together toward the Third Millennium," added new clarity and focus by asserting that it is the local church which is "the acting subject of mission."

"The renewal of our sense of mission will mean...that the acting subject of mission is the local church living and acting in communion with the universal Church. It is the local churches and communities which can discern and work out (in dialogue with each other and with other persons of goodwill) the way the Gospel is best proclaimed, the Church set up, the values of God's Kingdom realized in their own place and time. In fact, it is by responding to and serving the needs of the peoples of Asia that the different Christian communities become truly local churches" (FABC V, 3.3.1).

"This local church, which is the acting subject of mission, is the people of God in a given milieu, the whole Christian community—laity, Religious and clergy. It is the whole diocese, the parish, the Basic Ecclesial Community and other groups. Their time has come for Asia" (FABC V, 3.3.2).

FABC VI. The Sixth FABC Plenary Assembly held in Manila in 1995 in conjunction with the visit of Pope John Paul II for the World Youth Day summarized key themes of the 25-year history of FABC. The final statement entitled "Christian

Discipleship in Asia Today: Service to Life" noted that: "The overall thrust of activities in recent years has been to motivate the Churches of Asia towards 'a new way of being Church,' a Church that is committed to becoming 'a community of communities' and a credible sign of salvation and liberation" (FABC VI, 3). "It is the Spirit of Jesus that creates the [Church as a] disciple-community" (FABC VI, 14).

Many are the challenges of being an authentic local church in Asia. Asian Catholics admit: "We may hesitate because we are a minority group. Indeed we are a little flock in Asia. But it is from this position of weakness that God's gift of divine life in Jesus Crucified, the power and wisdom of God, is most significant" (FABC VI, 14.3). Most local churches in Asia continually discover and live their identities as minorities within their national societies.

ASIAN SYNOD ECHOES FABC THEMES. A short excursus provides interesting insights into key FABC themes about local church that resounded in the Special Assembly for Asia of the Synod of Bishops ("Asian Synod") held in Rome from April 18-May 14, 1998. As Cardinal Stephen Kim Sou-hwan of Korea greeted the Holy Father and the Synod participants in his opening address on April 20, he described the realities of Asia which "is made up not of various nations but, one may say, many worlds."

Kim noted the endeavors and accomplishments of the FABC "for the past 27 years"; in building up a truly local church in Asia "continual and quite serious efforts have been made to listen to, learn from, and reflect and act upon today's lived Asian realities in faith and prayer. And, we have felt called to an ever renewed self-understanding of the Church and her mission, not so much from abstract thought, but in the face of given pastoral situations and their exigencies" (OR-EE: April 29, 1998, p. 5).

Bishop Josef Suwatan, MSC of Indonesia asserted that the "peoples of Asia need the witness of 'being Church'." He pointed out how "the Fifth Plenary Assembly of FABC in 1990 in Bandung speaks about 'a new way of being Church' in Asia, as a 'communion of communities'." He reiterated: "Note well, it speaks about 'being' Church!" (OR-EE: April 29, 1998, p. 15). Again, Archbishop Petrus Turang of Indonesia echoed the same theme and focused on the growth of the local churches: "The Churches of Asia need to take advantage of the vision of a new way of being Church" (OR-EE: May 20, 1998, p. 8). This new approach will also achieve, according to Bishop John Cummins, "the desired communion among local Churches"; this means accepting "the Federation of Asian Bishops' Conferences as a vehicle to do this" (OR-EE: May 20, 1998, p. 13).

The missionary dimension of the local churches of Asia emerged strongly in the Synod. Father Edward Malone, FABC Assistant Secretary General, emphasized several crucial points: "Asian Christians and local Churches have a deep sense of gratitude for the gift of faith.... With the renewal of ecclesiology a wide variety of mission initiatives must necessarily emerge from within each local Church...." Concretely, specific actions must help promote "the emergence of missionary local Churches"; thus, "pastoral care is not to derail the local Church mission effort" and "the actual foundation of Asian-born missionary societies is to be fostered in each local Church" (OR-EE: May 13, 1998, p. 14).

Several Synod interventions focused on the challenges of this FABC-inspired "new way of being Church." Bishop Pakiam of Malaysia captured the essence of this commitment to "be witnesses of the Gospel as a community of the local Church in a multiracial, multicultural, multilinguistic country"; note that this description reflects the reality of most Asian countries. Bishop Pakiam recommended following FABC directions so that local churches become "a communion of communities, a partici- patory Church, a dialoguing and prophetic Church" (OR-EE: June 17, 1998, p. 8).

In the final session of the Synod on May 13, Cardinal Darmaatmadja of Indonesia again referred to the task of "being Church in Asia." For him all local Churches must struggle to be "a Church with an Asian 'face' [and an] Asian appearance"; they must avoid appearing "foreign to Asia's traditions and cultures" (OR-EE: June 17, 1998, pp. 10-11). In a word, they must emerge as truly local Churches!

THEMATIC RECAPITULATION. This presentation has briefly sketched the development of reflection on the local church in Asia over the past quarter century. The eminent Asian theologian, Catalino G. Arévalo, S.J., has recently reflected on the growth of Asian local churches in the *Jahrbuch für Kontextuelle Theologien* 1995 [1995 *Yearbook of Contextual Theologies*]. His insights in this document are worthy of extensive citation.

He notes that since the renewal of Vatican II "the Church in the FABC region was seeking increasingly to '*become* Church'.... It was an exciting time to awaken minds and hearts of Asian Christians to the real endeavor of the 'self-realization of the Church'" (p. 32). Arévalo continues (pp. 33-34):

"For me, behind the desire for constructing local theologies [ecclesiologies] lies the 'dream of catholicity.' The catholicity of the Church has been a passion, in a way, in my mind and heart since my first contacts with ecclesiology.... It is a consequence of Incarnation and Paschal Mystery, it is the meaning of Pentecost, that (rightly understood) the realization of *catholicity* is the meaning of the Church's mission."

"That means that every people, every place in Asia, has a vocation to the realization of the catholicity of the Church. Christ is 'not yet complete' until all of humanity, each part of it, has made its contribution to the 'Christ of all peoples.' Every people has its gifts and riches, and the Father has a place for all these gifts, in the Kingdom, in the Body of His Son. Equality and participation is a calling for each people in the human family. Until each people has made the contribution to the Church's unity-in-diversity which it has a right and duty to make, the work of mission of the Church has not been fulfilled."

"My growing conviction has been that each place and region in Asia has to make its specific contribution to the mosaic which constitutes the catholicity of the Church, which in my mind is one of the most important principles of our faith. Every people has a right to find its place within the church. Every local church can only contribute to this *dream of catholicity* when it is given a status of equality and participation, because every people in the eyes of the Father is equal to all the others and has a right to be loved for themselves and for the gifts and particular contribution it can make."

"Catholicity implies that we all have need of one another. That is the ultimate meaning of local church for me. A local church is never a means in itself, but in equality and participation every local church helps to bring forth the catholic communion as the ultimate aim of being church."

"The Church catholic is a communion of local churches. Every local Church is a Church in a given time and place, but it is also in communion, both diachronically and synchronically, with the Church in all times and in all the world. Unless every local church shares in the *koinonia* that is the Church universal, in true equality, in authentic participation, in the interchange of gifts and blessings, the dream of catholicity has not yet been realized. It is part of our deepest duty, as Catholics especially, to help bring this to pass."

An interviewer framed this question for Arévalo: "You concentrate on the local church in Asia as the operative agent of mission; ...do you see Asian local churches living up to the ideal that every local church is called to be a missionary, called to be a 'sending Church'"? Arévalo responded (p. 35):

"On the local church, this I believe must be said again and again: the concrete, operative meaning of inculturation is the process of letting the local Church be the local Church, assuming responsibility, within the *koinonia* of all the churches in the *catholica*, to 'realize itself' in its own life and mission.... Until the local Churches see their own self-realization as their duty and task, and strive to bring this about, they have not yet 'become Church' in the truest, fullest sense. Yet here in Asia, we are still a long way from that"!

"The operative center of the Church's mission today is the local Church: it must discern for its own time and place what the concrete tasks of its own mission are.... We will make every effort at a renewed evangelization, but one that is truly inculturated and integral (in all dimensions of our common life). Most of our local communities are far from accomplishing these objectives."

Arévalo continues in an optimistic vein (Arévalo: B, p. 20):

"The past twenty years of the common journey of the Asian Bishops in FABC have been years of growth for our local churches, hopefully 'in wisdom, age and grace.' In the years ahead the tasks discerned for mission remain in front of us as challenges which we have only begun to meet. *Their doing remains.*"

CONCLUSION. The experience of the pilgrim local churches in Asia since Vatican II has been an exciting and inspiring faith-journey. It has been an experience in ecclesiogenesis, the birthing and development of local churches. It has verified the ancient adage that the church is always *in via*, on the road, in process—as she awaits her Lord and Savior, Jesus Christ. The road has not been a well-trodden path; Asian churches are making the pilgrim way in the very process of walking it—under the guidance of the befriending Spirit. Asian Christians are enthusiastic pilgrim-disciples; a renewed local church for a new world is being born in Asia.

Local churches, full of vitality through faith and the power of the Holy Spirit, will engage in reading the "signs of the times" (GS 4) and responding to concrete social, political, economic, religious, and cultural realities. They will foster their own inner life (inculturated faith) and be better equipped to dialogue with other Christians (ecumenism) and the followers of other faith traditions (interreligious dialogue). In short, they will experience self-actualization and "see themselves as responsible agents for the self-realization of the Church" (TLC: C-4). They will experientially know that they are "the acting subject of mission" (FABC V, 3.3.1). They will rejoice in their "new way of being Church" (FABC VI, 3).

Each local church in Asia has received abundant and diverse gifts from the Holy Spirit. Each church is to give freely because it has received freely (cf. Mt. 10:8). In this manner each local church contributes to the realization of the catholicity of the church. To cite Arévalo, "Unless every local church shares in the *koinonia* that is the Church universal, in true equality, in authentic participation, in the interchange of gifts and blessings, the dream of catholicity has not yet been realized. It is part of our deepest duty, as Catholics especially, to help bring this to pass" (Arévalo: D, p. 34). Thus, the entire church becomes, as noted by Vatican II, the *corpus ecclesiarum* (LG 23), the body of the churches, the corporate body of local churches.

The church catholic is a communion of local churches; the church catholic is built upon the "principle of communion" as John Paul II noted in his message to the Catholics of China from Manila in January of 1995 (cf. PA:CC). Or again, in the Catholic experience, the more that each local church becomes truly inculturated, indigenized and localized, the more this same church through the power of the Holy Spirit becomes universal. And, the dream of vibrant local churches within an authentic catholicity continues to grow and take on flesh. Christians frequently meditate on the wondrous mystery that in the power of the Spirit the Church is for believers *donum Dei atque officium nostri*, at one and the same time, both God's gift and our task!

ENDNOTES

[1] Two insightful introductory overviews of the evolution, work, and documents of the Federation of Asian Bishops' Conferences can be found in the first compendium of FABC materials entitled *For All the Peoples of Asia - I*, pp. xv-xxx; consult the bibliography for detailed references to this volume.

[2] This presentation uses a succinct, yet clear, method of documentation. All items quoted are identified with abbreviations and numbers: e.g. FABC I, 8; by consulting the list of abbreviations and the bibliography one would see that this refers to the First FABC Plenary Assembly and its document "Evangelization in Modern Day Asia," section 8. This approach is necessary because the documents of the FABC (like Vatican II) have been published in a wide variety of formats and languages.

[3] The author has chosen to present the FABC material on the local church in a chronological manner, because this format lends itself to greater clarity. A decision has also been made to quote the FABC materials directly and extensively; this approach avoids diluting the freshness, creativity, and insightfulness of the original documents.

SELECT BIBLIOGRAPHY ON LOCAL CHURCH

Almario, Cirilo (Ed.). *Evangelization in Asia* (Proceedings of the Asian Congress on Evangelization). Quezon City, Philippines: Claretian Publications, 1993.

Arévalo, Catalino. **[A]** "The Church as a Community of Faith," FABC *Papers* No. 29. Hong Kong: FABC Secretariat, 1982; **[B]** "The Church in Asia and Mission in the 1990s," FABC *Papers* No. 57b. Hong Kong: FABC Secretariat, 1990; **[C]** "Mission in the 1990s," *International Bulletin of Missionary Research*. Vol. 14, No. 2 (April, 1990), pp. 50-53; **[D]** "Self-Portrait: A Life in the Service of the Church in the Philippines and of Asia" (Interview by Georg Evers) in: *Jahrbuch für Kontextuelle Theologien* 1995. Aachen, Germany:

Missionswissenschaftliches Institut Missio e.V., 1995; pp. 7-52.

Dianich, Severino. *La Iglesia en misión, hacia una eclesiología dinámica*. Salamanca: Sígueme, 1988.

Doyle, Dennis. "Communion Ecclesiology," *Church* Vol. 12, No. 1 (Spring, 1996), pp. 41-44.

Evers, Georg (Ed.). *Bibliography on Local Church in Asia* (published as *Theology in Context Supplements*, Number 3). Aachen, Germany: Institute of Missiology, 1989.

Forte, Bruno. *The Church: Icon of the Trinity* (*La Chiesa, icona della Trinita* -1984) Boston: St. Paul Books and Media, 1991.

Gnanapiragasam, John & **Wilfred**, Felix (Eds.). *Being Church in Asia* (Volume I). Quezon City, Philippines: Claretian Publications, 1994; NOTE: This volume contains "Theses on the Local Church," pp. 33-89 (Abbreviation: TLC); see also FABC *Papers No. 60*.

Heyndrickx, Jerome. "The Emergence of a Local Catholic Church in China?" *Tripod* No. 37 (1987), pp. 51-75.

Komonchak, Joseph. **[A]** "The Church Universal as the Communion of Local Churches" in: Alberigo, G. & Gutierrez, G. (Eds.). *Where Does the Church Stand?* New York: The Seabury Press, 1981; pp. 30-35; **[B]** "Towards a Theology of the Local Church," FABC *Papers No. 42*. Hong Kong: FABC Secretariat, 1986; **[C]** "The Local Realization of the Church," in: Alberigo, G., Jossua, J-P., & Komonchak, J. (Eds.). *The Reception of Vatican II*. Washington, D.C.: The Catholic University of America Press, 1987; pp. 77-90; **[D]** "The Church: God's Gift and Our Task," *Origins* Vol. 16, No. 42 (April 2, 1987), pp. 735-741; **[E]** "The Local Church," *Chicago Studies* Vol. 28, No. 3 (November, 1989), pp. 320-335; **[F]** "Many Models, One Church," *Church* Vol. 9, No. 1 (Spring, 1993), pp. 12-15.

Kroeger, James. *Living Mission: Challenges in Evangelization Today.* Maryknoll, New York: Orbis Books and Quezon City, Philippines: Claretian Publications, 1994.

LaRousse, William. *Urgency for Mission in the Local Church* [Licentiate Thesis in Missiology]. Rome, Italy: Gregorian University, 1997.

LaVerdiere, Eugene. "Local Churches in a Universal Church," *Origins* Vol. 19, No. 5 (June 15, 1989), pp. 65-71.

Parappally, Jacob. "Communion among the Individual Churches," *Vidyajyoti Journal of Theological Reflection* Vol. 59, No. 11 (November, 1995), pp. 753-761.

Rosales, Gaudencio & **Arévalo**, Catalino (Eds.). *For All the Peoples of Asia: Federation of Asian Bishops' Conferences Documents: I - II.* [Abbreviation: FAPA]. Maryknoll, New York: Orbis Books and Quezon City, Philippines: Claretian Publications, 1992 and 1997.

Salm, Luke (Ed.). *Proceedings of the Thirty-Sixth Annual Convention.* Bronx, New York: The Catholic Theological Society of America, 1981; NOTE: The entire volume is devoted to "local church" as its central theme.

Schreiter, Robert. "The Theological Meaning of a Truly Catholic Church," *New Theology Review* Vol. 7, No. 4 (November, 1994), pp. 5-17.

Seigel, Michael & **Mercado**, Leonardo (Eds.). *Towards an Asian Theology of Mission.* Manila: Divine Word Publications, 1995.

Tillard, Jean Marie Roger. *Church of Churches: The Ecclesiology of Communion (Église d'Églises - 1987)* Collegeville, Minn.: The Liturgical Press, 1992.

Zago, Marcello. *Volti della Chiesa in Asia.* Milan, Italy: Edizioni Paoline, 1990.

ABBREVIATIONS

ACMC - Asian Colloquium on Ministries in the Church (Hong Kong - 1977) in: FAPA - I pp. 67-92.

FABC - Federation of Asian Bishops' Conferences.

FABC I - Evangelization in Modern Day Asia (Taipei, Taiwan - 1974) in: FAPA - I pp. 11-25.

FABC II - Prayer—The Life of the Church in Asia (Calcutta, India - 1978) in FAPA - I pp. 27-48.

FABC III - The Church—A community of Faith in Asia (Bangkok, Thailand - 1982) in: FAPA - I pp. 49-65.

FABC V - Journeying Together Toward the Third Millennium (Bandung, Indonesia - 1990) in: FAPA - I pp. 273-289.

FABC VI - Christian Discipleship in Asia Today: Service to Life (Manila, Philippines - 1995) in: FAPA II pp. 1-12.

FAPA - *For All the Peoples of Asia:* I. Edited by: Rosales, Gaudencio & Arévalo, Catalino. Maryknoll, New York: Orbis Books and Quezon City, Philippines: Claretian Publications, 1992; *For All the Peoples of Asia:* II. Edited by: Eilers, Franz-Josef. Quezon City, Philippines: Claretian Publications, 1997.

GS - *Gaudium et Spes* (The Church in the Modern World: December 7, 1965).

IMC   -   International Mission Congress (Manila, Philippines - 1979) in: FAPA - I   pp. 125-163.

LG   -   *Lumen Gentium* (The Church: November 21, 1964).

OR-EE -   *L'Osservatore Romano* (English Edition)

PA: CC -   Papal Address to Chinese Catholics (John Paul II - January 14, 1995) in: OR-EE Vol. 28, No. 3 |1374| (January 18, 1995), p. 1.

TAC   -   Theological Advisory Commission of the FABC.

TLC   -   Theses on the Local Church; document prepared by TAC and published in: Gnanapiragasam & Wilfred, pp. 33-89.

CHAPTER 11

ASIAN MISSIONARIES: CONTACT INFORMATION

Fr. Manuel C. JADRAQUE, Jr., MSP
Mission Society of the Philippines
9105 Banuyo Street - San Antonio Village
Makati / Metro Manila PHILIPPINES

Tel. (63-2) 896.1634
524.2977
(63-2) 524.2979
FAX: (632) 524.2995

Fr. Thomas PARAYADYIL, MST
Missionary Society of St. Thomas
MST, Deepti Bhavan
Melampara - 686594 - Kerala, INDIA

Tel. (91-482) 236.353
237.653
237.453

Fr. Bonaventura JUNG, KMS
Korean Foreign Mission Society
1 Ga 120, Sung Buk Dong
Sung Buk Gu, Seoul KOREA 130-021

Tel. (82-2) 3673.2525
766.3172

FAX: (82-2) 743.7002

Rev. Dr. Jose KAIMLETT, HGN
Heralds of Good News
Tallapalem Post Office
Machilipatanam 521 002 INDIA

Tel. (91) 8672-42213

FAX: (91) 8672-42214

Fr. Jean DANTONEL, MEP
Mission Society of Thailand
Lux Mundi Seminary
20 Petchkasem Road - Sampran
Nakornpathom 73110 THAILAND

Tel. (66-2) 429.0820

FAX: (66-2) 429.0819

Msgr. Paul LU, PME
Lorenzo Ruiz Mission Society
San Carlos - EDSA - Guadalupe
M. C. P.O. Box 1414
1254 Makati City, Metro Manila
PHILIPPINES

Tel. (63-2) 895.8855
(local: 450)
(63-2) 895.9062

FAX: (63-2) 890.9561

Fr. James H. KROEGER, MM
AMSAL Secretary - Convenor
Maryknoll Box 285
Greenhills Post Office
1502 Metro Manila, PHILIPPINES

Tel. (63-2) 426-6101
722-4952

FAX: (63-2) 426-6112
722-4952

BOOKS BY J. H. KROEGER

THE PHILIPPINE CHURCH AND EVANGELIZATION: 1965-1984.
Rome, Italy: Gregorian University Press, 1985.

ADVANCED CEBUANO COLLOQUIAL EXPRESSIONS.
Davao City, Philippines: Institute of Language and Culture, 1986.

CHURCH TRULY ALIVE: JOURNEY TO THE FILIPINO REVOLUTION.
Davao City, Philippines: Mission Studies Institute, 1988.

KNOWING CHRIST JESUS: A CHRISTOLOGICAL SOURCEBOOK
Quezon City, Philippines: Claretian Publications, 1989.

INTERRELIGIOUS DIALOGUE: CATHOLIC PERSPECTIVES
Davao City, Philippines: Missions Studies Institute, 1990.

MISSION TODAY: CONTEMPORARY THEMES IN MISSIOLOGY.
Hong Kong: Federation of Asian Bishops' Conferences, 1991.

LIVING MISSION: CHALLENGES IN EVANGELIZATION TODAY.
Maryknoll, New York: Orbis Books, 1994.
Quezon City, Philippines: Claretian Publications, 1994.

CONTEMPORARY MISSION ISSUES.
A series of eleven pamphlets on mission issues.
Maryknoll, New York: Maryknoll Press, 1995-1997.

REMEMBERING OUR BISHOP JOSEPH W. REGAN, M.M.
Quezon City, Philippines: Claretian Publications, 1998.